SURVEY
OF
EARLY AMERICAN
DESIGN

Other volumes in the
ARCHITECTURAL TREASURES
OF EARLY AMERICA
Series

SURVEY
OF
EARLY AMERICAN
DESIGN

Vol. I in the Architectural Treasures of Early America Series

From material originally published as
The White Pine Series of Architectural Monographs
edited by
Russell F. Whitehead and Frank Chouteau Brown

Lisa C. Mullins, Series Editor

Preface by Roy Underhill,
Master Housewright at Colonial Williamsburg

A Publication of The National Historical Society

DISTRIBUTED BY

THE MAIN STREET PRESS • Pittstown, New Jersey

Copyright © 1987 by The National Historical Society

Published by
The National Historical Society
2245 Kohn Road, Box 8200
Harrisburg, Pennsylvania 17105

Distributed by
The Main Street Press
William Case House
Pittstown, New Jersey 08867

Distributed simultaneously in Canada by
Methuen Publications
2330 Midland Avenue
Agincourt, Ontario M1S 1P7

Printed in the United States of America

10   9   8   7   6   5   4   3   2   1

Library of Congress Cataloging-in-Publication Data

Survey of Early American design.
    (Architectural treasures of Early America; 1)
    1. Architecture, Colonial—United States.
2. Architecture—United States. 3. Architecture—
Details. I. Mullins, Lisa C. II. Underhill, Roy.
III. Series: Architectural treasures of Early America
(Harrisburg, Pa.); 1.
NA707.S94   1987   720'.974   87-7442
ISBN 0-918678-20-X

The original photographs reproduced in this publication are from the collection of drawings and photographs in "The White Pine Monograph Series, Collected and Edited by Russell F. Whitehead, The George P. Lindsay Collection." The collection, part of the research and reference collections of The American Institute of Architects, Washington, D.C., was acquired by the Institute in 1955 from the Whitehead estate, through the cooperation of Mrs. Russell F. Whitehead, and the generosity of the Weyerhauser Timber Company, which purchased the collection for presentation to the Institute. The research and reference collections of the Institute are available for public use. A written request for such use is required so that space may be reserved and assistance made available.

CONTENTS

PREFACE

During the years of the Great War, with Bauhaus ("Forget the past!") just around the corner, young architects discovered America. Suddenly they were competing with each other to express the beauty of American wood, rather than European stone. "We were searching for the best of the past to incorporate into the design of today," recalls one architect involved in the restoration of Colonial Williamsburg. And the best of the past became The Monograph Series, the premier sourcebook of early American architecture.

These were the wild young days of architectural history and preservation. Frank E. Wallis, in his 1916 monograph on the houses of the Southern colonies, told of sailing up the York River to the ruins of Rosewell "in a log dugout." "How we got there I do not know." He admitted bribing a "complacent tenant to watch for the landlord" while he and his cohorts removed an early staircase from a North Boston home. They carried off the "beautiful twisted newel-post with the varying carved balusters and mahogany rail" leaving a cheap replacement in its stead.

The editors of The Monograph Series knew what they were doing. "Appreciating that most architects prefer to form their own conclusions from good photographs, the pictorial side of the work will be made the dominant feature," noted Whitehead in the introduction to the series. These photographs are superb documents. Technically excellent, you can pick out the details of the work, and see the light and shadows on mouldings. These photographs record early American buildings, many now lost, in close to their original condition and environment. (Look for the giant American elms and chestnut trees, now largely gone.) But these photographs are more than just documents. They are also classics of architectural photography, thoughtful compositions with a strength of light that calls us to sit again on these sunny porches.

And the drawings are superb; the work of professional draftsmen. Their job was not to design a building, but to perfect its expression on paper. In those days, there was a great emphasis on drawing, due in part to the technical requirements of the printing process. The renderings in The Monograph Series were executed in a manner that would reproduce exceptionally well. Although there are still people who can do this quality of work, few people think that they can afford it. Standardization has cut a wide swath through the architectural trades. If you are going to resort to a millwork catalogue and simply pick out acceptable windows and doors, then there is no point in spending time drawing specifications. We gain a little and we lose a little, and try to save the best.

Yet the drawings and photographs are only the surface. The authors of The Monograph Series understood the flesh and bones of these buildings. "Wood to these old men was a servant, and they played in and out through the grain of the woods," wrote Whitehead, "in such fashion as would have shocked the stolid Britishers of the Georgian times." Some hewed to the texture of the old work as well: one owner "has built his home in the form of the early period, leaving the marks of the adze and other implements on the wood, following the old methods of construction carefully, the result being a modern house thoroughly American in spirit and of old-time honesty and charm of feeling."

These homes, the children of The Monograph Series, have now taken their place in the history around us. In towns around the country, you can spot the winners of the annual awards for the best traditional designs in white pine. Built throughout the 1920's, these homes provided roots for a society that was creating giant superfunctional boxes to work in. These homes have their own story; a grand heritage worth preserving.

Those charged with preserving this heritage are responsible to both the past and the future. Ed Kendrew was one of the architects with the firm of Perry, Shaw and Hepburn that began the restoration of Colonial Williamsburg in the 1920's. For he and his colleagues, The Monograph Series was a sourcebook and a standard. "We always had them handy," he recalls. "We were missing a few of the earlier issues and searched everywhere to try and find them."

Even though Williamsburg is in the South, the buildings of The Monograph Series helped to define the regional style of Tidewater Virginia. "The differences between what we were used to in New England and what we found in the South were extremely exciting," Kendrew remembers. "It made a challenge of all of our study, our climbing into torrid attics, wet basements and broken down floors that might collapse on us." The Monograph Series was, and is, an invaluable tool for those who strive for a restoration that they can "back with precedent, and with knowledge of good craftsmanship."

The best things last, and the *White Pine Series of Architectural Monographs* is back.

ROY UNDERHILL
MASTER HOUSEWRIGHT
COLONIAL WILLIAMSBURG

HISTORICAL INTRODUCTION

Being a pioneer is not always as rewarding as nostalgia, fond recollection, and forgiving memory often make it seem. Those who go first are all too often forgotten, neglected, or misunderstood, except by a very few whose unique perspective puts them in a position to appreciate what a pathbreaker has achieved. In all probability, that is how Russell Whitehead and his associates felt in their later years. By the 1960's, their pioneering work in recording early American architecture was all but ignored in the resurgence of "olde colonial" and "country" building. At best, we can hope that they found some amusement in seeing the presentation of "colonial" split-levels or "Georgian" ranchers in the developers' prospectuses.

Better than that, we can hope as well that they felt some inner satisfaction in knowing that at least a few—architects, architectural historians, true students and lovers of the genuine early American genre—still treasured the work, still tended the flame which they had lit in those days long before when the *White Pine Series of Architectural Monographs* made history by recording history. In that quarter century, from 1914 to 1940, in its varying formats and under several guiding hands, The Monograph Series never lost sight of its original mandate—to record and preserve for posterity, as well as for emulation, the architectural treasures of early America.

That they did, but unfortunately their work reached only a limited audience, though one upon which it had a profound effect, as Roy Underhill so tellingly reveals in his Preface to this volume. Distribution of the monographs was small, many—perhaps most—copies did not long survive, and today the majority of collections of them are in public libraries or private architectural firms, many of them incomplete collections at that.

Yet one would have to be blind not to recognize the telling relevance of these works to the America of today, a nation avidly looking backward to retain what it still can of its architectural heritage, and reaching even farther to try to recover what has been lost. All across America individuals and communities are working with dedication toward those ends. Ironically, having emerged from a generation or two in which "new" meant "best", we find ourselves today aggressively proud of the notion that "old" is "good" where our buildings are concerned, and the older the better. At the same time, we have emerged from the stylistic fog of the "split-level-colonial-rancher" days to a new appreciation of genuine, authentic, documented architectural detail, and a desire to recreate it in our living and working places.

In such a climate, the need for those old monographs is transparent. For one thing, they contain a wealth of information, especially visual, on hundreds of early American buildings as they appeared prior to sometimes intrusive or anachronistic "restoration." Better still, for many structures the Monographs are the only remaining record of buildings that have since fallen victim to fire, demolition, or other manmade or natural destruction.

It is that clear need, and the interest which it serves, that has led to *The Architectural*

9

Treasures of Early America. In this and the volumes to follow you will see what has hitherto been available only to a few architectural historians and designers—photographs, precise measured drawings, and informative and often amusing text, which open to laymen and professionals alike an opportunity to appreciate the craftsmanship of our forebears, as well as to recreate the stunning architectural features which give early American homes their distinctive character. Here, in these volumes, we present anew The Monograph Series, doing for it—we hope—what the Series itself did for the buildings of our ancestors.

The first issue of The Monograph Series appeared in 1914, to the delight of many architects. Originally begun as an advertising device, The Monograph Series soon took its place as the most comprehensive work ever produced on early American architecture. The White Pine Bureau, comprising the Northern Pine Manufacturers' Association of Minnesota, Wisconsin, and Michigan and the Associated White Pine Manufacturers of Idaho, sought to "further acquaint the architect with 'White Pine—Its Qualities—Its Availability—Its Cost' through The Monograph Series. By presenting "classified illustrations of wood construction, critically described by representative American architects, of the most beautiful and suggestive examples of architecture old and new, which this country has produced," the Bureau hoped the series would "earn a place as a valuable addition to the literature on architecture and thereby become worthy of preservation in a library of standard architectural works."

The Bureau engaged noted architect Russell F. Whitehead as editor of the series and Julian Buckly as the architectural photographer. Since one of the series' objectives was to stimulate awareness among architects of white pine's importance as a building material, the editors placed certain restrictions upon the subject matter. Only residences built of white pine would be covered, and then only their exteriors.

For ten years the series continued under these guidelines until 1924, when the White Pine Bureau stopped all advertising—including The Monograph Series. Not wishing to discontinue such a popular and significant architectural reference, Whitehead devised a means of continuing the series as an independent enterprise. To defray the editorial and printing costs, Weyerhauser Forest Products agreed to act as sponsor, buying four pages of advertising in each issue. Both parties decided to illustrate Weyerhauser's advertisements with photographs and drawings related to each monograph's subject matter.

Noting that the previous monographs had certain biases created by the strictures placed upon the material, namely a focus on New England because this area had remained virtually unchanged and displayed a preponderance of white pine houses, Whitehead decided now to alter the series focus. No longer would it be "confined to the publication of residence work." Henceforth "a monograph on any little town [would] show it completely, including such of its old churches or public buildings as still remain, and with photographs of both interior work and minor architectural accessories." Nor would "it be necessary to restrict [the] photographs to buildings chiefly constructed of white pine . . . thus it [would] be possible to illustrate some of the charming work still existing in the southern states." The Monograph Series continued in this new direction until 1932, when it was absorbed into *Pencil Points*, a monthly magazine for architectural draftsmen, and there it appeared as a regular feature until its abrupt termination in June 1940, never to reappear.

There was an undeniable charm to The Monograph Series that lasted throughout its twenty-six years. Almost without exception, the photographs were wonderful, taken by Julian Buckly, Kenneth Clark, and Arthur C. Haskell, each architectural photographers of national reputation. The measured drawings, many of them from the pen of Frank Chouteau Brown and Ken Clark, are models of the craft—precise, detailed, and yet artworks in their own right. It is no wonder that the WPA eagerly accepted the contributions of Brown, Haskell, and others connected with the monographs, when it began the collection of photographs and drawings from all across the country for the landmark Historic American Buildings Survey, a notable architectural endeavor which continues to this day. Indeed, it is not too much to say that the H.A.B.S. collection which, now resides in the Library of Congress and with various state agencies, is in many ways an offspring of the work already under way since 1914 thanks to The Monograph Series.

The text for the monographs, often from the pens of the architects or photographers who provided the illustrations, varies as much as the personalities of the men and women themselves. Some are matter of fact, some are witty, a few simply tell an interesting local story or two while illustrating the buildings. These people were *architectural* historians, not historians in the general sense of the term, and thus sometimes their background on people and events may stray from the facts as we know them today. But their photographs and drawings cannot be questioned. They show us in unmistakable images, the look of early America.

Of course, the editors did pay a modest fee, at least in the early days. According to Aymar Embury, author of a number of the first articles, the promised fee was $50 per monograph, "and sometimes I even got paid!" Compensated or not, they did it for the love of the doing, and of the buildings they preserved. That same affection burns today, perhaps brighter than ever before. Drawn to that light, the editors of the National Historical Society recognized the lasting relevance of the old Monograph Series for the preservation and restoration movements of today. To serve that end, to make available to architectural historians once more this significant and practical series, and to present it as well to a general interested public who never had access to the originals, we have created *The Architectural Treasures of Early America*.

How to go about re-issuing a series like the monographs presents quite a puzzle. Under varying editors and publishers, the individual articles appeared in a number of different typefaces, page sizes, and design styles. Simply to reprint them as is would have led to an annoyingly disjointed appearance, especially given our decision not to reprint the monographs in the order in which they originally appeared. Since they followed no set pattern as they came out one after another, any one volume combining, say, two or three years' worth of monographs would present a subject matter hodge-podge. Consequently, we decided at the outset to reorganize the monographs, along geographic lines, with books on the Southern states, seaside New England, and so forth.

This first volume, *Survey of Early American Design*, and the final two volumes vary from this format by focusing on specific architectural features rather than regional architecture.

Solving that problem, however, led to another, for now any one volume might combine monographs from 1914, 1925, 1933, and up to 1940. Here the differences in design and print would become blatantly distracting. This, then, led to the decision to completely reset the text of the monographs in a new, uniform type throughout, choosing the typeface used when they first began to appear in 1914. At the same time, this allowed us to correct a few typographical errors that crept into the originals, as well as to add comprehensive cross-references to other articles throughout the series. Nevertheless, in setting the type we took special pains to ensure that most pages of *The Architectural Treasures* will read word-for-word exactly as the original. Further, we have preserved precisely the design of the monographs, all of the illustrations in place, and the design of each page unvarying from that of its "ancestor." Because through its history, a number of appealing formats and special design features came and went in The Monograph Series, we have chosen those which we found most appealing and used them uniformly throughout. We have even decided to print the volumes in a pleasing shade of green ink used in some of the early Monographs.

The result of all this effort, we feel, is to lend to *The Architectural Treasures of Early America* something which even The Monograph Series lacked; a sense of order and continuity throughout, helping to open the wonderful contents of each volume to the general reader interested in learning more about our architectural heritage, without compromising in any way the inestimable value of the original content of the monographs to the architectural professional.

The most difficult problem of all was the illustrations. The measured drawings present no difficulty at all. They reproduce today just as clear and dramatic as they were in the originals. The photographs, however, are another story. The state of halftone reproduction in the 1910's was not what it is today, and even many of the monographs published as late as the 1930's did not offer very high quality printing of the images. Without having the actual photographs to work with, we would have no choice but to reproduce them from the printed pages of the monographs themselves, thus putting us one generation further from the original artwork, and risking the additional lack of reproductive quality which that entails. Until a few months before going to press, this appeared to be our only alternative.

But then months of fruitless searching for the originals were at last rewarded. We discovered that in 1955, Russell Whitehead's widow, with very little fanfare, turned over his papers and almost 3,000 photographs to Weyerhauser Forest Products who then gave the collection to the American Institute of Architects in Washington, D.C. There they sat, largely unknown and entirely unused, until January 1987 when we first examined them. We were overwhelmed. While not all of the images actually used in The Monograph Series are there, perhaps as many as one third are, and the balance of the collection consists of hundreds of unused photos of early American buildings which offer a treasure trove to future historians. Thanks only to the extraordinary assistance of Archivist Tony Wrenn, who rushed the processing of the collection so that we could copy the photos, and to the generous cooperation of Timothy Hargrove and the directors of the AIA in allowing us the use of them, are we able in this and succeeding volumes to reproduce many of those old photographs with a clarity and sharpness of detail otherwise unattainable. Indeed, in some cases it is even better than they appeared in the monographs themselves. As for the balance of the photos, we have experimented with a variety of printing processes to produce the best reproduction possible. And as the years unfold, and later printings of these volumes become necessary, we may well be able to substitute yet more original photos for the reprints, for there are tantalizing leads in the Whitehead collection which may yet lead us to the balance of the actual photographs used.

Meanwhile, there are others whose efforts deserve our special thanks, even as this work continues. Our photographer Ken Smith performed wonderfully in the copying of the fragile, and sometimes faded or damaged, original images at the AIA. Our typesetter worked diligently to preserve the typeface and styles of the original. Our designer Deborah Bond patiently and calmly lived with us through one incarnation after another of the design, as we evolved by trial and error toward our final presentation. And to our friend Roy Underhill, Master Housewright at Colonial Williamsburg, we owe special regard for the charming, witty, informative prefaces which so perfectly set the tone for each of the volumes.

Most of all, of course, we—and all who read, view, and use *The Architectural Treasures of Early America*—owe enduring gratitude to Russell Whitehead, Frank Chouteau Brown, Julian Buckly, Kenneth Clark, Arthur C. Haskell, and all the others who shared the vision of The Monograph Series. Thanks to them, Americans of today and for all time can share a priceless glimpse of our architectural heritage, both that lost and that preserved. In it we can see the industry and vitality of a young America as it built its homes and churches and taverns and mills, and with them, a nation.

WILLIAM C. DAVIS
PRESIDENT
NATIONAL HISTORICAL SOCIETY

SURVEY
OF
EARLY AMERICAN
DESIGN

Early Wooden Architecture in Andover, Mass.

Text by
Addison B. LeBoutillier
Photographs by
Julian A. Buckly
Originally published in 1917 as White Pine Monograph
Volume III, Number 2

Detail of Doorway and Entrance Porch

PHELPS (OR "PRESIDENT'S") HOUSE — 1809–1812 — ANDOVER HILL, MASSACHUSETTS

This view shows the delicate detail of the fluted porch columns and
architraves, the turned bed moulds and carved Doric entablature.

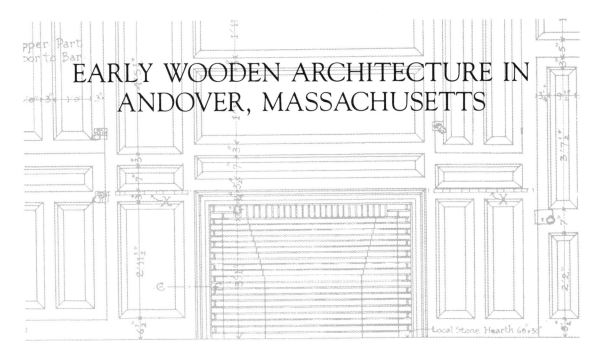

EARLY WOODEN ARCHITECTURE IN ANDOVER, MASSACHUSETTS

THE towns of Andover and North Andover, situated in the valleys of the Merrimac and Shawsheen Rivers and occupying about one-sixth of the territory of Essex County, are historically and architecturally interesting, as since their foundation in 1646 they have been typical of New England tradition and civilization.

The early settlers, coming from Cambridge, Salem, Ipswich and Rowley, were a hardy, thrifty and pious people, many of whose dwellings fortunately remain to reflect their prosperity. Therefore, in this community may be traced, by existing examples, the development of New England wooden architecture, from the humble farmhouses of the seventeenth century to the stately mansions of one hundred years ago.

From the original settlement of scattered farms the town grew and prospered, in spite of hardships, Indian wars and the witchcraft frenzy. Many of the citizens became rich, as riches were counted in those days, and with their wealth came comforts, leisure and learning of the true New England type. "The town had a grammar and district school, two churches that were crowded on Sunday and weekly lecture days. There was a social library in the North Parish and on the whole the town of Andover was as flourishing as any inland town of the Commonwealth."

In 1778 Phillips Academy was founded, and some years later Andover Theological Seminary. These were established upon Andover Hill, at that time a rocky upland pasture. Around this

nucleus there grew up in the space of fifty years a remarkable group of houses, whose occupants left names well known in history, literature and theology. Here, in 1782, Judge Phillips, the founder of the Academy, built his fine three-story "mansion house"—which, until its destruction by fire, was the finest house on the Hill. The finest remaining house, and one of the show places on the Hill, is the "President's House," built for Dr. Griffin, at that time president of the Seminary. It appears that the donor, Mr. William Bartlet, of Newburyport, gave Dr. Griffin *carte blanche*, and, happily for us, he took him at his word, for the result, as will be seen by the illustrations (opposite and page 25), is an exceptionally fine example of wooden architecture. Even the detail view of the porch and doorway gives little idea of the scale of this design. It may, perhaps, be partially grasped by noticing that the screen door is cut a couple of feet below the top of the opening— that being evidently considered as providing ample height for ordinary occupants to pass in and out—as indeed it does! The proportion of the house is so well kept, the detail of the porch and house cornice, the arched windows and doors, so delicate and beautiful, that the spectator is unable to realize the unusual height of the story— unusual even at the comparatively late date of this example.

The two towns were formerly one (originally called "Cochichawicke"), the first settlements being at what are now called North Andover and "Frye Village," where more examples of houses of the olden type are to be found.

Of course the Governor Bradstreet House in North Andover is one of the most famous of early Massachusetts dwellings. While many of its rooms have been repaneled and ceiled, one or two still retain the old English type of paneling that proves its great antiquity. Only its somewhat retired location prevents this house from being far better known than it is,—especially as it lies almost across the street from

the same year as the house, presumed to have been begun immediately after the former dwelling was destroyed by fire in July, 1666. Tradition states this was the home of Simon Bradstreet, who came to America with Governor Winthrop in 1630 and was one of the first settlers of Andover. He built the first mill on the "Cochituate," near its junction with the Merrimac River, in 1644, thus founding the milling industries of Lawrence, Massachusetts. He afterwards returned to Salem, when he is supposed to

GOVERNOR BRADSTREET HOUSE — 1667 — NORTH ANDOVER, MASSACHUSETTS

Built by one of the first settlers of Andover, Simon Bradstreet, afterwards Deputy Governor and Governor. It was also the home of the first woman poet of America, Anne Bradstreet, and survived several Indian raids. The sash in the lower windows are not original.

the old Phillips House, with its entrance doorway set off-center of the façade, and its unusually capacious and hospitable gambrel slopes,— a dwelling which would be of interest to many tourists because of its associations with Phillips Brooks. To architects it may—perhaps—serve as some palliation to record that the present end veranda was added by the late H. H. Richardson.

The Bradstreet House is the only dwelling now existing from the first fifty-year period of Andover's settlement. Its frame is of massive timbers, its walls are lined with brick, and the two huge elms in front are supposed to date from

have relinquished this house to his son, Col. Dudley Bradstreet, as the dwelling was certainly known to belong to him until his death in 1702.

In the "South Parish," now the town of Andover, is the Abbot Farmhouse, standing beside the old brook—*and* the newer railroad embankment—at the left of the track just as the train approaches the Andover station. With its service courtyard thrown out around the wonderful old elm that overhangs the road, it makes as beautiful and picturesque an old New England farmhouse as can anywhere be found —despite the fact that the old brick of the

OLD ABBOT FARM HOUSE — 1685 — ANDOVER, MASSACHUSETTS

chimney has since been plastered and the old window sash removed or changed.

Of the gambrel roof type of house this locality furnishes numerous examples, many of them with that short upper slope which seems always to provide a certain quaintness of aspect. This is to be noted in three or four of the present illustrations—in one case, at least, in the earlier type with small windows, and in another and later example (shown on page 23) with an unusually fine and sturdy hand-worked cornice.

Even the small Colonial cottage is represented

along the range of sheds added at the rear. This Swift House is itself a particularly sturdy and successful example of later Colonial type, with its interesting monitor roof treatment and virile detail. The same sturdy character of detail appears in the Abbot House doorway on Central Street, with the Greek fret worked into the soffit of the pediment of the cornice and its squat bellying frieze. The Newman House, on Andover Hill, possesses an especially well worked out order, and the entrance and second-story Palladian window archway are enriched by

PHILLIPS HOUSE — 1752 — NORTH ANDOVER, MASSACHUSETTS

Built by the Honorable Samuel Phillips. The porch covers two end doorways, both with pediments and toplights. The one in the center of the gable also had pilasters and supporting brackets. The smaller door, just at the back wall, had only a surrounding architrave but boasted eight panels.

by a charming example—now a tea-room—in Andover village; while the old Abbot tavern, with its historical associations, although it has now little of the exterior aspect of its previous use, yet preserves two examples of that particular local type of outer vestibule, frequently to be found in Andover, where, apparently, the side arched window was a favorite touch of some late colonial builder.

Not only this tavern but the little tea-room and the old Swift House on Central Street both carry this type of arch at the sides of the vestibule. In the latter house it is also worked into the pediment over the entrance door, as well as

ornamental patterns carefully grooved by a carpenter's gouge in the way that is often found in local work.

Andover also provides several examples of the three-story house type, of which the Kittredge House is the only instance that has been utilized in this chapter. At the time of its construction this house had no equal for elegance in the whole "North Parish," and it was rivalled only by Judge Phillips's mansion, then recently built—and since destroyed—in the "South Parish." "The lofty ceilings, great hall and broad staircase, heavy door and ponderous brass knocker, the avenue of trees leading to the front entrance, still mark it as a stately home, of a courtly period when the aristocratic ideas of old-country traditions still held in the style of living and social customs of the Colonies."

Oddly enough, despite the fact that there still exist in Andover so many old dwellings, no one of the several early houses of worship built by the settlers has come down to the present day. The first "meeting house" is supposed to have been built near the old "North Burying Ground," where in 1669 a "new meeting house" was built "with upper and lower galleries," and another church was built in 1709 in the Andover "South Parish." This last church stood until 1734, when a second building was erected and occupied until 1787, along with a parsonage — a gambrel roof house now occupied as a private residence. Although not illustrated in this chapter, its quaint construction long made it one of the most interesting of old Andover houses. Unfortunately, this meeting house was demol-

ished in 1835, the porch removed to the manufacturing village near the Merrimac and fitted up as part of a dwelling house, while the pew walls made a unique fence in the front yard of a neighboring house, west of the common.

However, all the old churches have disappeared, and so only the old dwellings of the town — many more examples than it was possible to illustrate in these pages — remain to provide an architectural background into which can be read the history of a New England farming community and its gradual progression from prosperous early colonial to more recent times. Fortunately, the modern tremendous milling industries that settled in this district — making Lawrence so famous and ugly! — chose newer sites, and so the portly old farmhouses of the several earlier scattered settlements have been spared to delight us with a virile architectural beauty that we can appreciate even while we fail in equalling it today!

COL. JAMES FRYE HOUSE — 1725 — NORTH ANDOVER, MASSACHUSETTS

The windows, and perhaps the porch, are more modern. A huge elm — a famous
landmark planted in 1725 by Chaplain Frye — stood near this house until quite recently.

OLD ABBOT TAVERN — 1740 — ANDOVER, MASSACHUSETTS

PHELPS HOUSE (OR "PRESIDENT'S" HOUSE)—1812—ANDOVER HILL, MASSACHUSETTS
A stately and refined dwelling built by William Bartlet of Newburyport.

MANNING HOUSE ON PORTER ROAD — 1758 — ANDOVER, MASSACHUSETTS

COL. SAMUEL JOHNSON HOUSE — NORTH ANDOVER, MASSACHUSETTS

This house was built by Capt. Timothy Johnson, and given by him in 1771 to Col. Samuel Johnson, his son.

OLD HOUSE — ANDOVER, MASSACHUSETTS
Squire Jno. Kneeland occupied this house about 1796. Exact date of building unknown.
It is a charmingly informal cottage, now known as the "Rose Cottage Tea Room."

KITTREDGE HOUSE — 1784 — NORTH ANDOVER, MASSACHUSETTS
Built by Dr. Thomas Kittredge, surgeon in Col. Frye's regiment. Attributed to Samuel McIntire.
At the time the walls of this house were "raised," Dr. Kittredge had colored slaves as servants.

Doorway

GEORGE ABBOT HOUSE—1796—ANDOVER, MASSACHUSETTS

Entrance Porch

MARK H. NEWMAN HOUSE—1824—ANDOVER HILL, MASSACHUSETTS

OLD SWIFT HOUSE — 1795 — ANDOVER, MASSACHUSETTS

"Mr. Swift has raised his house and partly boarded it, which is all that's new among us that
I can think of." Extract from a letter of 1795 that establishes the date of this structure.

Detail of Side Doorway and Vestibule
OLD SWIFT HOUSE — 1795 — ANDOVER, MASSACHUSETTS

An unusually fine example of the type of vestibule, with its small over-
arched side window, that is distinctive of, and local to, the town of Andover.

New England Inns and Taverns

Text by
Hubert G. Ripley
Photographs by
Arthur C. Haskell
Originally published in 1932 as White Pine Monograph
Volume XVIII, Number 6

Detail of Front Elevation
COLLIN'S TAVERN, NAUGATUCK, CONNECTICUT

NEW ENGLAND INNS AND TAVERNS

THE American Colonies were settled so rapidly that one of the earliest evidences of the new order was the establishment of a string of inns and taverns reaching from Massachusetts Bay to the Carolinas. The seaports, of course, had to provide accommodation for the constant stream of new arrivals, until they could find homesteads and build the lovely old houses, churches, court rooms, and town offices, many of which, so well were they designed and constructed, are still cherished monuments of seventeenth and eighteenth century culture. The Old State House in Boston and the old court room in Yorktown are splendid examples of the Georgian style, than which no finer exist any place.

The designations "Inn" and "Tavern" are used interchangeably, though in comparatively recent times "Tavern" has come to mean a place where food and drink were served to travelers, while "Inn" means that lodging also may be had. What fragrant memories cluster around the mention of "The Bell in Hand," and "The Old Elm," for example, "The White Horse Tavern" and "The Bunch of Grapes" in Kingston. It was in this latter hostelry that the great American cocktail, at first christened the cock's tail, was invented. Whether the original Bunch of Grapes is still standing, I scarcely know; probably it was destroyed when the British, under Sir Henry Clinton, burned the town in 1777. Anyhow the history of the cocktail (whether authentic or not is immaterial) is a poetic legend and so fraught with romance that the telling of it may not be out of place here. We are indebted to "The Bumper Book," New York, 1899, for the tale that runs as follows:

Squire Allen, bluff and hearty, face a deep *bois de rose* o'erspread with indoor tan, dispensed good cheer to all comers at the aforesaid Bunch of Grapes. None need leave the tavern thirsty whether possessed of the medium of exchange or not, for mine host kept a blackboard behind the bar, on which the customer's score was chalked up when specie or barter lacked. Good ale and strong drink flowed freely, and the Squire's buxom daughter, Betty, assisted her father in caring for the wants of the guests. When the stage coach from Albany arrived and the driver pulled in his foam-flecked horses, it was a busy time for them both, and Betty, her apron strings fluttering in the fresh breezes, her rosy cheek "like a Catharine pear, the side the sun shone on," as Sir John Suckling puts it, skipped lightly from table to table under the old apple tree with pewters of ale, trays of glasses, bowls of loaf sugar and water from the Old Well Sweep. Her father followed, a wicker covered demijohn under one arm, a black bottle of Sour Mash in hand, and a merry greeting for all.

When Leftenant Titheridge, with his hardy recruits, tall gallant fellows recently returned from the Plains of Abraham, appeared one day, and drew up his squadron in the yard between the early American wagon sheds with their row of elliptical arches, and the great hay barn, Betty was at the Well Sweep.

"Halt!" cried the gallant officer.

"Allow *me!*" were his words, and dismounting quickly he strode with rapid strides across the intervening space to the well, flinging his reins to Sargent Simpkins as he did so.

"What a lovely spot!" he added. "I think we'll stay here a while and rest up a bit. You look tired."

As he spoke these words, his muscular arms manipulated the well sweep and, despite Betty's protestation, he carried two full buckets of ice cold water into the kitchen with the ease and familiarity bred of active outdoor life combined with the grace of manner that betokened a gallant soldier not unfamiliar with the salons of the quality.

"Oh sir!" said Betty, dropping him a curtsy, "I thank you. You must be awful strong!" and she blushed prettily and looked down in modest confusion.

"*Du tout!*" replied the leftenant lightly, for he spoke French fluently, and was fond of displaying his knowledge. In the midst of the slight embarrassment caused by the unexpected meeting of two extremely attractive young people of opposite sex (such an embarrassment would be most unusual nowadays, it may be said) the Squire appeared.

His face was like a thundercloud, the cause of which was not long in appearing. It seemed that the Innkeeper was greatly addicted to the sport of cock-fighting and inordinately proud of his prize cock Excalibar, whose valour and skill in the cock-pit were renowned throughout the countryside. The exploits of this lusty fowl had gained not only a redoubtable reputation for its owner as a trainer and sportsman, but had also resulted considerably to his pecuniary advantage. Many envied him the possession of such a paragon, and, indeed well they might for never before in three counties had been seen such noble courage, finer breed, and staying qualities than displayed by this young hero of many a cocking main. His age was three years and seven months and he tipped the scales at 4 lbs. 14 oz., a very knight among birds with a plumed tail worthy of Agamemnon's crest. For two days Excalibar had been missing, the Squire had hunted for him high and low throughout the neighborhood and among his corn cribs. Nowhere could a trace of him be discovered. The prince of birds had been stolen!

Leftenant Titheridge looked thoughtful as he recalled a half-forgotten incident of the hike down the river, but he said nothing. It was solemn and dismal cheer for the guests that night at the Bunch of Grapes. Shortly after daybreak the next morning the young officer rode away, bidding his men await his return. Everyone at the Tavern was disconsolate. Even Sargent Simpkins, a fine upstanding young man with a prepossessing face, and an eye for a pretty girl, scarce remarked the nimble figure of the Innkeeper's daughter as she busied herself with her household duties, sweeping the taproom, sanding the floor in graceful arabesques, plucking green corn, and tending the marigolds and johnny-jump-ups, for her garden was the delight of all visitors. Night drew on apace and no leftenant appeared. Again a gloomy and dismal meal while the candles guttered unsnuffed and the Squire smoked pipe after pipe, refusing all conversation.

As dawn, the rosy fingered, came peeping o'er the hills, Sargent Simpkins felt a touch on his shoulder.

"*Qui va la?*" he muttered sleepily, for he had picked up a smattering of French during the hardships of the Quebec campaign.

"*Je,*" whispered the voice of Leftenant Titheridge, for it was indeed none other. He held something indistinguishable in the half light. It was Excalibar unharmed and in all the glory of his plumage, brilliant as when the rays of the rising sun tip with iridescent glow the towering walls of the Fred F. French Building on Fifth Avenue, or the first view of the 1933 Chicago World's Fair startles the astonished visitor.

The sensitive ear of Squire Allen, a light sleeper, caught the whispered conversation in the adjoining room, and slipping quickly into his small clothes, he pushed open the door. Catching sight of his matchless bird, he uttered a great shout that aroused the entire household. Soon the room was filled with a joyous throng of guests, retainers and soldiers. Even Betty, with a green joseph thrown hastily over her night rail, peeped shyly in with admiring glances at the handsome young officer who, after searching far and wide, had returned triumphant with his quarry. Fully recovered from the spleen and black humor of the past three days, the overjoyed host called for the best breakfast the house afforded, while Betty slipped off hastily to put into execution an idea of her own. Let us quote an extract from the tale itself.

"Now whether it were from excitement or nervousness, or whether, perchance, mistress Daisy had before discovered the secret, and held it close for a great event, certain it is that she mixed sundry drops of bitters and wine of roots, with a dram of good Kentucky whisky, the whole poured over some generous bits of ice (not a little luxury in itself), and they all drank of the beverage "to the cock's tail"—for Jupiter had not lost a single feather. And then the gallant leftenant sware bravely that, in memory of the event, the delectable mixture he had drunk should be known as a cock's tail through all the army."

[Note: The author seems a bit confused. He calls the charming inventor "Betty" instead of Daisy, and the gallant cock "Excalibar" instead of Jupiter. *Ed.* Well, maybe I did, memory plays us pranks at times, but what of it? *Author.*]

The subsequent adventures of Leftenant Titheridge and Betty [he means Daisy, *Ed.*] is not strictly concerned with the subject of New England inns and taverns and need not be dwelt on further. Interested students and Antiquarys will find more of it in

RICE TAVERN, KITTERY, MAINE

RICE TAVERN, KITTERY, MAINE

COLLIN'S TAVERN, NAUGATUCK, CONNECTICUT

Detail of Front Elevation
WAYSIDE INN — 1686 — SUDBURY, MASSACHUSETTS

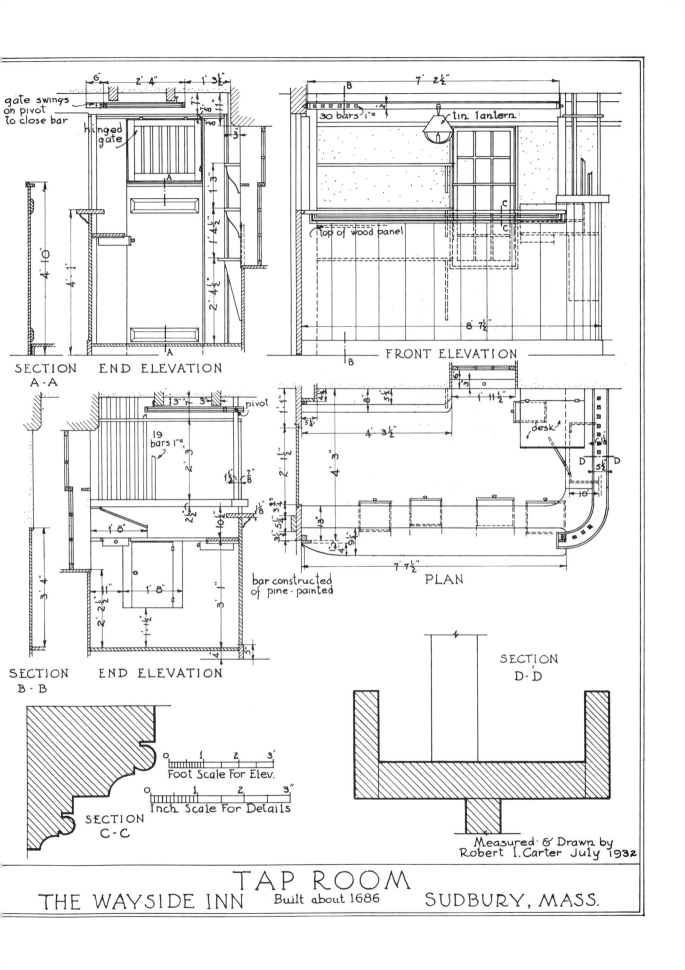

gate swings on pivot to close bar

hinged gate

SECTION A-A

END ELEVATION

B

7' 2½"

30 bars 1"□

tin lantern

top of wood panel

8 7½"

B

FRONT ELEVATION

pivot

19 bars 1"□

bar constructed of pine·painted

desk

D

D

4' 3½"

7' 7½"

PLAN

SECTION B-B

END ELEVATION

0 1 2 3'
Foot Scale For Elev.

0 1 2 3"
Inch Scale For Details

SECTION C-C

SECTION D-D

Measured & Drawn by
Robert I. Carter July 1932

TAP ROOM
THE WAYSIDE INN   Built about 1686   SUDBURY, MASS.

Tap Room and Bar

WAYSIDE INN — 1686 — SUDBURY, MASSACHUSETTS

the "Bumper Book," together with other timely knowledge.

One of our early recollections was a visit to the famous "Bell in Hand," located for over a hundred years in Pi Alley, Boston. This was strictly a tavern and no other beverage, not even water, was served save good stout ale. Brie cheese, cold meats, coarse bread and hot mutton pies were available for the modest sum of five cents for each item. A "half with a dash," was the customary order, meaning a half mug of ale with a dash of porter. The ale was Bass, imported in barrels, and besides this a very special brand called Union Ale, which was smooth as silk and strong as the Hercules of Lysippus. About three full mugs of Union and you felt as if slammed by the Hero's club. The porter was bitter without being acrid, and seemed like velvet to the tongue. When drunken with brie cheese, its full flavor could best be appreciated. Customers almost always ordered half mugs (nothing but pewter was used in the tavern, by the way) in the belief that two halves were greater than a whole, yet so canny was the skill of the burly tapsters who drew the precious fluid, great husky lads with mighty arms, that it was a toss up either way. We've tried the experiment several times and never found that two halves caused an overflowing when poured together.

Many famous men were the inn's customers, and while the place was severely simple, early American in character with wide pine boards and sanded floors, low ceilings and a few old prints on the walls, and while the clientele included almost every strata in our complex civilization from the highest to the lowly, I've never observed unseemly behavior or conduct that could be classed as an offense against good taste. When such men as Judge Palmer, the well-known authority on jurisprudence, Lieutenant Colonel Will, U.S.A., A.I.A., P.D., etc., etc., and Chelsea Joe, that polished devotee of the goddess of chance, patronize an establishment, one may safely follow in their footsteps.

Then there was "The Old Elm," a tavern that lent distinction and the aura of its personality to Tremont Street Mall in its declining years. This place was named from its proximity to the Washington Elm that grew opposite it on Boston Common. (The original Washington Elm was in Cambridge, of course, and the one on the common an offshoot from the parent stem.) Maybe there was once an "Old Elm" near the Cambridge tree, I don't know. Food was the main idea there, and the best *beer* in Boston, according to the local connoisseurs. We had our first glass of beer there when a student at Tech, and as I

recall the incident, I was not greatly overjoyed by the experiment. It tasted strange and bitter. Since then, experience and wisdom have demonstrated the many excellent qualities of this ancient beverage when used with discretion. Weisse beer was also served there in babble glasses, great huge mugs holding a gallon, like the famous *"formidable,"* at the "Brasserie Lipp."

"The Old Wayside Inn" in Sudbury is perhaps the best known of all New England taverns as the setting of the delightful tales of the lovable transcendentalist of the Golden Age. Though marred somewhat by the vandal hand of the great apostle of standardization and exploitation, it still retains much of its original charm when seen from certain view points, in spite of the absurdities of recent additions and strictures as to freedom of action imposed on its guests by the policy of its present owner. There are lovely old bedrooms, furnished right up to the last word of the present-day interior decorator's idea of just what an early American bedroom should be, many pieces of really good old furniture, and the old bar and dining room practically as was, as far as anybody knows. There are glass cases containing General Witherspoon's sword belt worn at the battle of Bennington, some old pewter, a spinning wheel in the front hall that tangles up people's feet and warming pans and trivets and trammel irons (whatever they are) galore; quite a store of junk when all is told. The front porch is punk, but the clapboards on the walls, still painted the same old exquisite shade of salmon pink it has always worn, and the sweep of the hospitable gambrel, are still worth going miles to see.

Many of the old inns, like the Wayside, are still doing a thriving business eight or nine months of the year, due to the motoring craze which is becoming popular again this fall. It really is great fun to drive through the brisk, snappy air of late autumn or early spring, or even through any air at all seasons, and find broiled chickens and candied sweet potatoes awaiting one. Some places they let you put the bottle right on the table, but mostly, on arrival, one has to sneak out behind the shed where they keep the harrows and the plow shares and say, "Here's how!" to the astonished cows. Not like the old days when they had real parties in these hallowed halls, beginning at two o'clock in the afternoon and lasting until breakfast time the next morning. Feasting and square dances and hard cider spiked with New England rum, and a bit of bundling perhaps, if the old records may be trusted. But dear me! here's the space all used up before the story's scarcely begun.

WILSON TAVERN — 1797 — PETERBOROUGH, NEW HAMPSHIRE

Tap Room

WILSON TAVERN — 1797 — PETERBOROUGH, NEW HAMPSHIRE

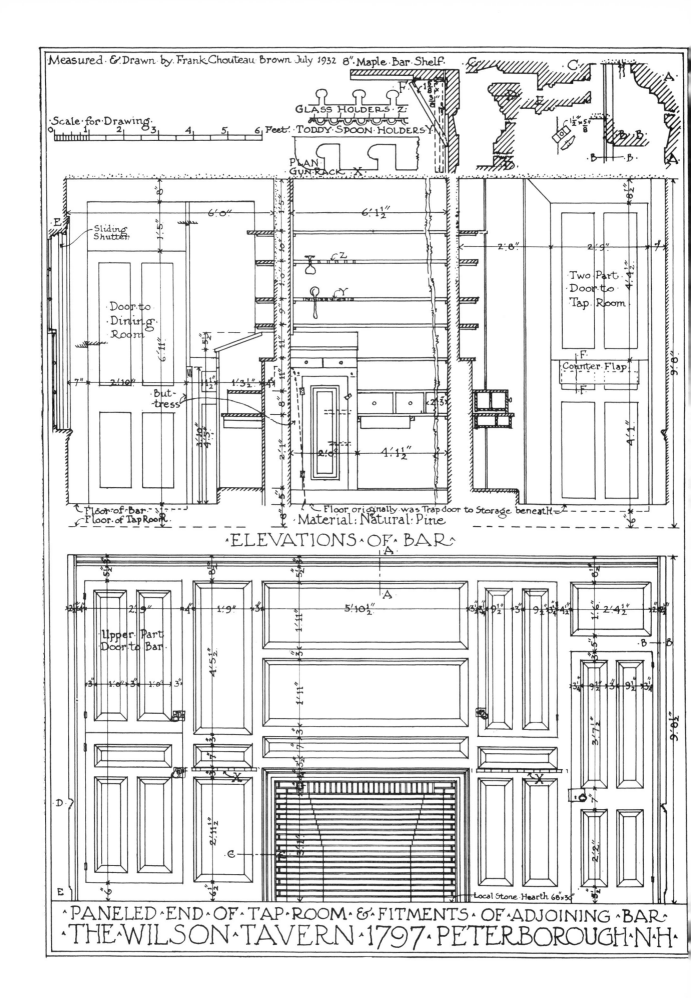

Measured & Drawn by Frank Chouteau Brown July 1932   8" Maple Bar Shelf

GLASS HOLDERS Z

TODDY SPOON HOLDERS Y

Scale for Drawing.

0 1 2 3 4 5 6 Feet.

PLAN
GUN RACK X

Sliding Shutter

Door to Dining Room

But-tress

Floor of Bar
Floor of Tap Room

Two Part Door to Tap Room

Counter Flap

Floor originally was Trap-door to Storage beneath

Material: Natural Pine

·ELEVATIONS·OF·BAR·

Upper Part Door to Bar

Local Stone Hearth 60"x30"

·PANELED·END·OF·TAP·ROOM·&·FITMENTS·OF·ADJOINING·BAR·
·THE·WILSON·TAVERN·1797·PETERBOROUGH·N·H·

OLD MILFORD TAVERN, MILFORD, NEW HAMPSHIRE

TAVERN — 1774 — WEST TOWNSEND, MASSACHUSETTS

OLD MILFORD TAVERN, MILFORD, NEW HAMPSHIRE

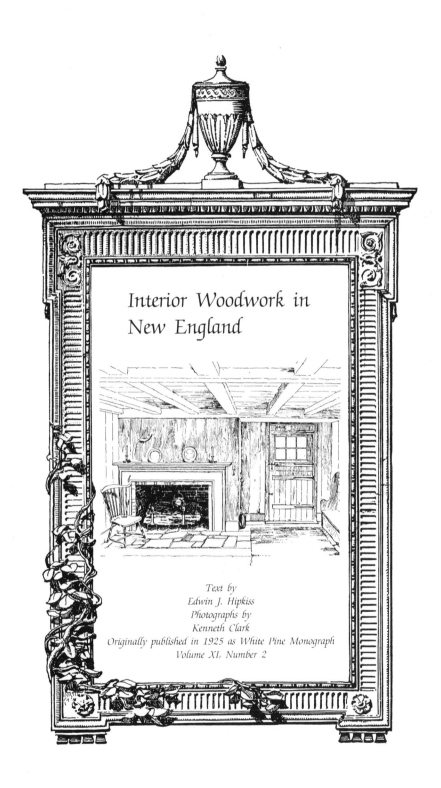

Interior Woodwork in New England

Text by
Edwin J. Hipkiss
Photographs by
Kenneth Clark
Originally published in 1925 as White Pine Monograph
Volume XI, Number 2

Stair Hall
VERNON HOUSE — 1758 — NEWPORT, RHODE ISLAND

INTERIOR WOODWORK IN NEW ENGLAND DURING THE SEVENTEENTH AND EIGHTEENTH CENTURIES

IN writing of our early interior woodwork, or in illustrating it, one feels a sense of restriction and a temptation to wander from the chosen topic into a treatment of old rooms as a whole. Obviously a room is not complete from an artistic point of view until it is furnished appropriately; old woodwork was but a part of that total effect. That there was a marked relationship, particularly in New England, between the character of architectural detail and the furnishings of the several stylistic phases is a fact needing wider recognition, since there is always the easy path of unrelated mixtures.

Nearly all our old rooms have suffered such losses, or accumulations, that both research and imagination are required to gather together once more their scattered elements, the effect of charm and decorative entity. Photographs and drawings serve as an introduction to old interiors but, it seems, one must actually enter a room to sense its scale, its proportions and the relation of one part to another.

Our earliest interiors, those of the seventeenth century, represent a folk-art, medieval in character. By the beginning of the eighteenth century a new style was evolved and, due to the availability and use of builder's handbooks, a sense of style was recognized from Maine to South Carolina. Although we know changes in the handling of this style varied according to time and place, yet changes came slowly and young men were trained to do and to think in the ways that would be expected of them in their maturity. Every joiner, cabinet-maker, housewright, carpenter, or carpenter-builder of the eighteenth century worked in the style of the time freely interpreted. All moulded work from the cornice of a high chest to the cornice of a mansion was cut by hand with planes formed to make the curved elements of this simple architecture of classical origin. There were quarter-round, half-round, ogee, scotia, cyma forms, etc., in planes of graduated sizes and these formed the keyboard upon which the designer or master workman played his endless variations.

In the woodwork of both the seventeenth and the eighteenth centuries the element of craftsmanship is important. The work of intelligent men, proud of a manual skill passed on from master to apprentice or from father to son, produced an ever fresh handling of well-known forms that were acceptable to several generations.

The architect of the present day may easily have a passing thought of envy in considering the directness, the coordination of artistic ways and means, that existed here in the eighteenth century. A scheme of interior woodwork had be be but sketched in a rough way, by the man who knew what he was about, and there were trained workmen all ready at hand with an established method and an ability to translate general ideas into finished work. To be sure they used and understood a limited architectural expression but, according to their needs, they mastered it and that, perhaps, is why we respect an inheritance of their work which makes up in genuineness what it may lack in "impressiveness" or costliness.

For our purpose, four general divisions in this early woodwork may be made: The work of the seventeenth century and three phases of the eighteenth century: early, middle and late. The woodwork of the seventeenth century and that of the eighteenth sprang from separate architectural traditions; the earlier work had a kinship with the smaller provincial buildings, still Gothic in origin, of sixteenth century England. Our woodwork soon after the year 1700 was wrought in the Anglo-classic style but in New England it bore the stamp of a certain American independence.

Eighteenth century woodwork was truly "finish" in the present-day sense of the word; it was a lining whereas the work of the seventeenth century was structural, an integral part of the building. Interiors of the seventeenth century displayed their corner-posts, girts, summer-beams and rafters with a frank acceptance of the structure. This exposed framing, mostly of oak, with its sound joinery is peculiarly attractive in our less robust and economical times. As a general rule, sheathing was placed against interior partitions in random widths of white pine and moulded bands were cut on each edge. These "shadow moulds," aside from their decorative value to the room, helped to enrich the line where the boards met in halved joints. There are also instances of the use of such sheathing applied horizontally.

Doors were of the batten type, often of two vertical boards moulded at the joint, with cross battens near the top and bottom and such doors with their wrought iron hinges, latches and faceted nail heads have a simple attractiveness and charm. In fact rooms of this early period with their mellowed tones of grayish-brown, their straightforward use of material simply adorned, their sturdy joinery and huge fireplaces have a rough honesty and strength which appeal to us, at times, as do old ships framed of oak and with an appearance of readiness for all weather—fair or foul.

For our second division there are the rooms of the earlier part of the eighteenth century in the new style with chimney breasts, dadoes, and even whole walls paneled with a breadth and simplicity in keeping with a general sense of design seen also in the furniture and silver of the time. Although walls were sometimes enriched with a pilaster treatment, the detail in both pilasters and cornices has a certain restraint and quietness that differentiates it from similar work of the mid-eighteenth century. This is well indicated in a room in the Webb House at Wethersfield, Conn., illustrated on page 58.

A general lack of mantel shelves is characteristic of these earlier rooms; bolection mouldings framed the fireplace openings and were also used to frame doorways and the wall panels. Doorheads were often semicircular in form and shell-top cupboards belong especially to this period. It seems necessary to add that against comparatively simple woodwork, decorative richness was gained in the occasional use of the popular "japanned furniture," and the general use of colorful needlework and other textiles.

In New England during the mid-eighteenth century there is evidence of a richer and bolder treatment of interior detail in keeping with the vigorous handling of furniture design then indebted to the school of Chippendale. There was a more elaborate treatment of the chimney breast, now generally fitted with a mantel, and a use of carving, consoles, "eared" architraves, fuller and richer cornices and pediments both plain and broken. One thinks of carved furniture with claw and ball feet, varied and elaborate chair backs, sofas of generous proportions and looking-glass frames with scroll and broken pediment forms as representing the spirit of this period. This same vigor in form and decoration applies to the work of the silversmiths.

The mansion-houses of Maryland and Virginia had greater variety in interior woodwork at an earlier date than did the fine houses of New England.

The change in general taste is well seen in two important houses at Portsmouth, N. H., the Warner House (1728) and the Wentworth-Gardner House (c1760).

The drawing-room of the Warner House, for example, has large bolection mouldings surrounding the fireplace, and around the arched door frames, smaller bolection mouldings surround the raised panels. The cornice of few and stout members is without dentils or modillions—there is a bold simplicity. A similar room in the Wentworth-Gardner House of about 1760, has a fuller treatment of the cornice, one room has a full entablature, and the stair hall with much enrichment and variety of elements, has both a dentil course and modillions in its cornice. Doors are rectangular; the architraves are flattened and also "eared" in several rooms.

However, although we may form our impressions of the works of a time upon dated examples there is a reservation to be kept in mind. In towns remote from the great centers they were slow to change and old tradition held on and a house with all the appearances of having been built about 1730 in the vicinity of Boston or Newport may be as late as 1750 in the valley of the Connecticut River.

The interior woodwork of the last quarter of the eighteenth century and of the early years of the nineteenth had attained a refinement, and at times an attenuation, which differed in the extreme from all earlier work. This was the time of subtlety and sophistication in design and not only planning but the attempt to visualize a result on paper became the aim of the planner of these later houses. Many fine houses of an earlier time had been outlined in a casual way by the owner and with general instructions for the parts such as "to be finished like Curnall Smith's loer rume." Much was left to the eye of the builder. In these later rooms, however, details and proportions were carefully studied in a drawingboard manner.

Such woodwork formed the natural background for refined furniture in the style of Heppelwhite or Sheraton, for delicate mirror frames, fine porcelain and silver with elegance and grace both in its form and its engraving.

Moulding forms had changed from the profiles adapted from the simpler orders to quirk-moulds of fine scale; there were delicate beading, elliptical sections and areas. An ornamental treatment was evolved by forming running patterns of gouge cuts and small borings usually in the frieze of a cornice. Toward the end of the century modelled reliefs in French putty were applied to mantelpieces, doorheads and cornices and this method of "putting on style" probably caused others before us to refer back to "the good old days." However, from the vantage point of an additional hundred years or more we see in this unassuming work of the eighteenth century three old essentials of good architecture, "a regard for Beauty, Necessity and Tradition."

Stair Hall
WEBB HOUSE — 1753 — WETHERSFIELD, CONNECTICUT
Built for Joseph Webb, circa 1753

Interior

THOMAS LEE HOUSE — 1660 — EAST LYME, CONNECTICUT

Interior

BURNHAM HOUSE — 1638-1670 — IPSWICH, MASSACHUSETTS

Interior
NOAH WEBSTER HOUSE — 1676 — WEST HARTFORD, CONNECTICUT

Interior
OLD SHIP TAVERN — 1675 — ESSEX, CONNECTICUT

WEBB HOUSE ("HOSPITALITY HALL") — 1753 —
WETHERSFIELD, CONNECTICUT
Main Entrance Detail

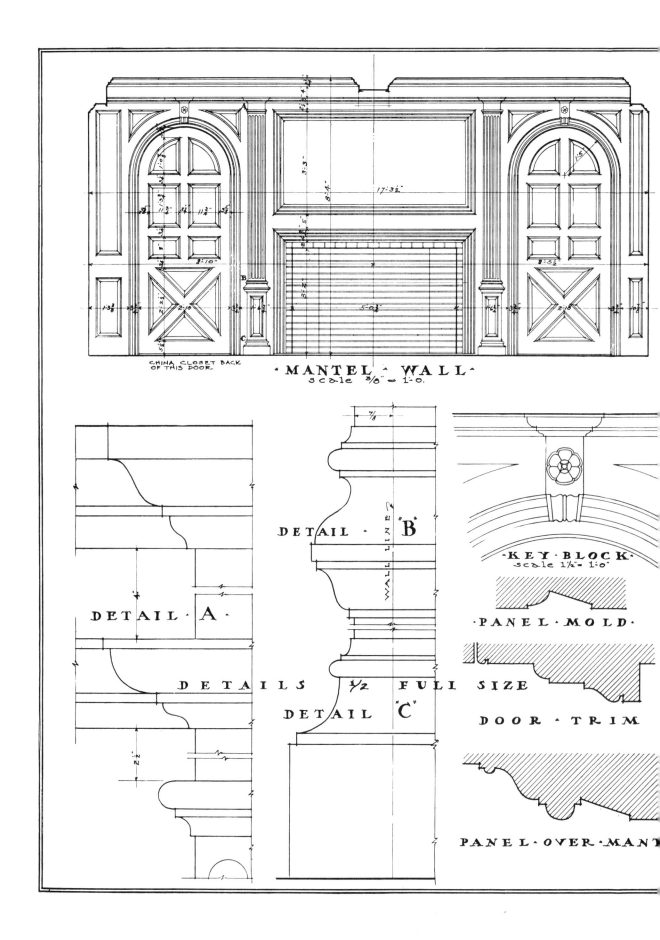

CHINA CLOSET BACK
OF THIS DOOR

·MANTEL·WALL·
scale ⅜" = 1'-0.

DETAIL·A·

DETAILS ½ FULL SIZE

DETAIL·"B"

DETAIL "C"

·KEY·BLOCK·
scale 1½" = 1'-0"

·PANEL·MOLD·

DOOR·TRIM

PANEL·OVER·MANT

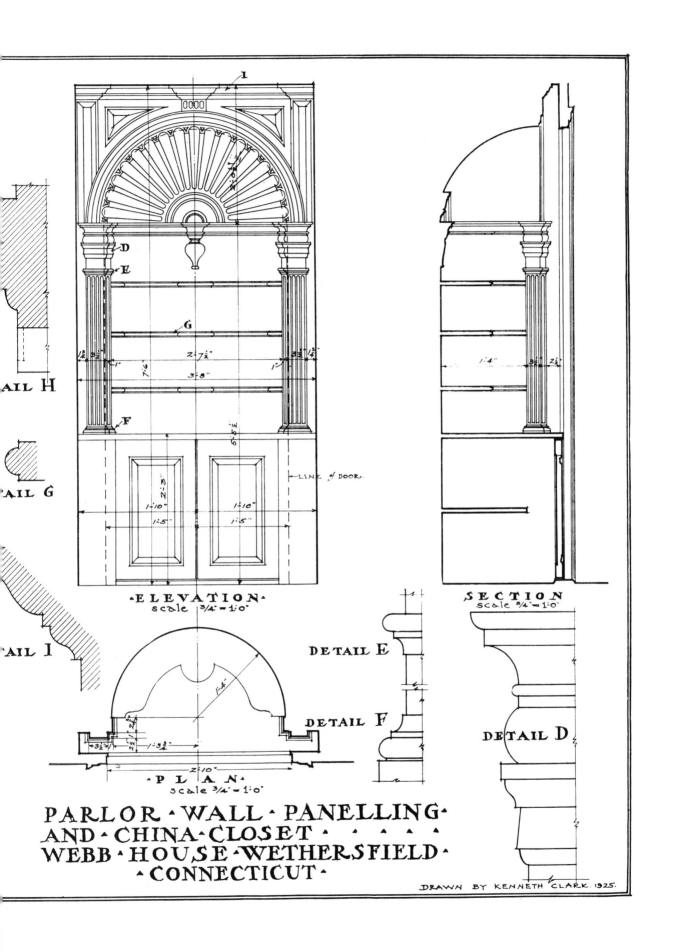

I

DETAIL H

DETAIL G

DETAIL I

D
E

G

2-7½"

3-8"

7-6"

F

5-5½"

LINE of DOOR

1-10"   1-10"

1-5"   1-5"

·ELEVATION·
scale ¾"=1'-0"

1'-4"   2½"

SECTION
scale ¾"=1'-0"

DETAIL E

DETAIL F

1-4"

2-10"

·PLAN·
scale ¾"=1'-0"

DETAIL D

PARLOR · WALL · PANELLING ·
AND · CHINA · CLOSET · · · ·
WEBB · HOUSE · WETHERSFIELD ·
· CONNECTICUT ·

DRAWN BY KENNETH CLARK. 1925.

North East Room — First Floor Parlor

WEBB HOUSE — 1753 — WETHERSFIELD, CONNECTICUT

Dining Room

WEBB HOUSE—1753—WETHERSFIELD, CONNECTICUT

Washington Chamber

WEBB HOUSE — 1753 — WETHERSFIELD, CONNECTICUT

Corner Cupboard
WEBB HOUSE, WETHERSFIELD, CONNECTICUT

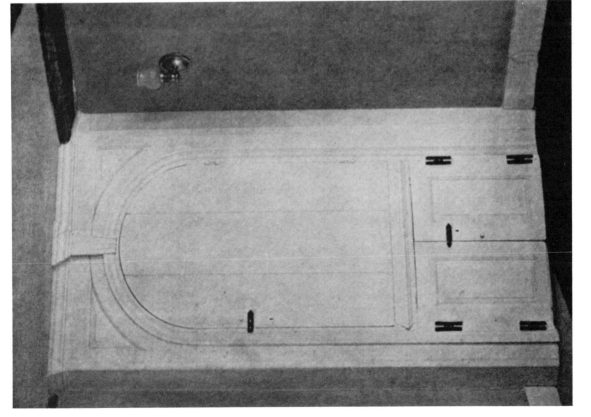

Corner Cupboard
MORRIS HOUSE, MORRIS COVE, CONNECTICUT

Living Room
GEN. EPAPHRODITUS CHAMPION HOUSE — 1794 — EAST HADDAM, CONNECTICUT

Early American Ornamental
Cornices, Part One

Text by
Aymar Embury II
Photographs by Kenneth Clark
Originally published in 1924 as White Pine Monograph
Volume X, Number 2

Detail of Cornice
BACON HOUSE — 1810 — KENT, CONNECTICUT

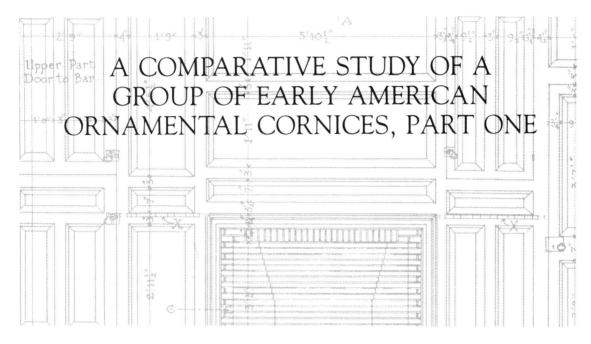

A COMPARATIVE STUDY OF A GROUP OF EARLY AMERICAN ORNAMENTAL CORNICES, PART ONE

*"CORNICE—A large moulding which forms the coping of a façade or portion of a façade, — or surmounts a door, window, dresser, etc."*ADELINE'S ART DICTIONARY.

This is one definition of a cornice; it is *not necessarily* part of an entablature copied from Vignola.

THE early American house was in nine cases out of ten a square box-like structure of clapboards or plain shingles with a decorative doorway and an ornamental cornice as the sole relieving features of a design otherwise simple to the point of meagerness. On the remaining tenth of the houses, the most usual additional decoration was the superposition of small cornice-like heads to the windows, which tended only slightly to distinguish these houses from those with plain window trims; and the houses in which the whole façade was consciously "designed" constitute an incredibly small minority of the whole group. A cursory examination of the back files of *The White Pine Series of Architectural Monographs* will not confirm this statement, but anyone familiar with the parts of the country from which the examples illustrated have been culled, will realize that the editor has missed few houses which contain something of particular individuality, while he has foregone photographing many houses of excellent design, the publication of which would be of interest only as records, and to the architect would be a needless repetition.

Even within such narrow limits of design as were set for the colonial architects by their materials, the general poverty of the country, and the lack of training of the architects themselves, they managed to achieve a surprising variety in their houses, a variety evidently only capable of accomplishment by slight changes in the proportions of the masses of the buildings, and by the use of different decorative motives in the design of the two focal points of interest, the doorways and the cornices. That they were not without originality is amply proved by the amazing number of different solutions that they were able to discover, and this in spite of the fact that their design was *always* based on classic motives as interpreted by the Renaissance architects, and not (as at present) modified by knowledge of practically all historic styles. In part their freedom from the dominance of the dead hand of Vignola was certainly due to sheer ignorance; ignorance not so much of books, as of the fundamentals of architectural drawing which would enable them correctly to understand the illustrations, a fact which is amply proved by the many cases where the builder obviously tried to imitate drawings and failed in the same way that an ignorant contractor today fails to understand the meaning of detail sheets. Examine for example the cornice illustrated on page 66 in which the general form of the Greek Doric order is approximately imitated, although no portion of it (and especially the triglyphs) is either clearly comprehended or correctly executed.

Cornice Detail of Entrance Porch
POST ROAD TAVERN, WESTMINSTER, CONNECTICUT

Ignorance however, was but one and probably not the dominant factor in producing such free design; the colonial architect was rather part of an architectural period than a copyist or interpreter of a past period, and was therefore totally unconscious of the need of consistency (if such need exists) which constantly hampers our modern designer; he never ran back to his collections of illustrations to see if others had done before him what he wanted to do; he probably had a certain amount of respect for precedent, but it was for precedent from which he could develop new motives, and not precedent as a storehouse containing all useful architectural motives.

The earliest form of cornice in America was really not classic at all, (above) but derived from the English cottage, with which it was contemporaneous, and the plain treatment of the eaves (it can hardly be called a cornice) was continuously in use in very cheap work especially in the country districts, where either lack of funds or lack of technical skill in the carpenter made a built up, molded and decorated cornice impossible. This treatment persisted throughout colonial times, as is illustrated by the Hempstead House at New London, Connecticut

Detail of Gable End
CAPEN HOUSE, TOPSFIELD, MASS.

Detail of Cornice
HEMPSTEAD HOUSE, NEW LONDON, CONN.

(below), and the Webb House at Orient, Long Island (pg. 68) built more than one hundred and fifty years apart; and today in small, cheap work in the outlying districts we find precisely the same method of terminating a roof, used for the same reasons.

Aside from houses with these overhangs, practically every house built before, let us say 1790 had a cornice of strictly classic genesis of not much originality and in itself of little interest however excellent it may have been as a crowning motive. These cornices, (and detail in general) closely followed English motives, or rather English adaptations of classic motives, slightly decreased in scale as befitted the material, and as a rule pretty well proportioned to the masses of the buildings. Where mistakes in scale occur they are usually in the direction of overscale rather than the reverse, due perhaps to imperfect digestion of the English precedent, and failure to realize that the proportion of cornice to wall should be determined by the material and general scale of the surface as well as by height. From the earlier cornices we have little to learn which is not in Vignola; examine the Vernon House at Newport, Rhode Island, built in 1758 (pg. 70) and the Burbank House at Suffield, Connecticut, built in 1736 (pg. 71) and it will be seen that we have in both cases typical classic cornices with consoles, in one case with a dentil course below. There is no motive not ordinarily found in England at the same time and while these whole cornices may be admirable crowning motives of the wall, they have no particular reason for illustration except as they explain the progress of the style.

by the use of pilasters against the wall, the frieze is entirely absent and the architrave suggested only over the pilasters with no corresponding breaks in the cornice or even the bed molds. The designer evidently had an idea which he did not quite know how to execute, but naïve as it is, it is nevertheless far more interesting than the correct cornices shown on pages 70 and 71.

Detail of Cornice
WEBB HOUSE, ORIENT, LONG ISLAND

On the other hand the Shirley-Eustace House at Roxbury, Massachusetts, built about 1750 (pg. 69) has a very distinct character of its own. The corona is entirely absent, the soffit beginning under the bead at the bottom of the cymatium; practically all the bed moldings are decorated with combinations of historic motives as unexpected and curious as they are pleasing; and although an entablature would seem to be required

When we come to examine the cornices of houses built after 1790 we find that the genuinely classic cornice is as rare as it was common in earlier times. A simple succession of run moldings continued to make up the crowning motive of the plainer and cheaper houses, but on the larger and more ornate there was no limit to the play of fancy, or rather there was no limit within the means of execution by ordinary carpenters' tools.

It must be remembered in studying colonial work that there were no power planes—all run moldings were got out by hand—there were few capable wood carvers, and composition ornament for outside work was unknown. The tools with which the ornaments were executed were few and simple, but the extraordinary variety of designs which were executed, with gouges and molding

Now while the discussion of the sources of American design applies to all portions of the buildings, it is of especial force as regards the cornice, since as the use of cornices as methods of ornamentation became more and more extended, not only was the intersection of the roof and the wall treated with a cornice, but the doors, the window-heads, porches, rooms, mantels, mirrors

Detail of Cornice
SHIRLEY-EUSTACE HOUSE, ROXBURY, MASSACHUSETTS

planes and especially with augers is amazing. Ornament sawn out with key-hole saws or turned on a lathe and applied to the surface of the boards is not infrequently found, especially in later work but ornament which could be done by a multiple molding plane and finished by a chisel or a gouge is by far the commonest, is perhaps the most ingenuously used, and is usually the best in scale with the light and graceful cornices of the period.

and even cupboards, were terminated by cornices of distinctly architectural character, and with little difference in the types employed. A cupboard cornice and the main cornice of a house differed in scale but not in character, and at the end of the century this was not the solemn dignity of classic design, but the free and playful translation of the cabinet-maker; the one difference being that in furniture varicolored wood

Detail of Cornice
VERNON HOUSE — 1758 — NEWPORT, RHODE ISLAND

Detail of Cornice
CAPTAIN ABRAHAM BURBANK HOUSE — 1736 — SUFFIELD, CONNECTICUT

inlays were often used to simulate flutes, wreathes or rosettes while the architectural ornament was always in relief.

The peculiar furniture-like cornice is as apparent in the books as in the executed work; and apparently the writers felt that no distinction was necessary between cornices used for various purposes, since page after page of cornices are

men technically not very skillful but with what was apparently a genuine feeling for detail, we find results which are elsewhere and at other times unequalled. Take for example the house at Chatham Center, New York, built in 1798 (below). This is not by any means the best designed cornice of the lot, and though not especially selected, will serve excellently to illustrate the points above

Detail of Cornice
HOUSE AT CHATHAM CENTER, NEW YORK

shown, the accompanying descriptive text giving no hint as to the portions of the building to which the authors thought them most appropriate; and in other pages where designs for mantels, doorways and houses are shown, the cornices are shown blocked out only, with the instruction that whatever cornice is most pleasing in the preceding pages may be used.

Drawn, as they were, from such sources, by

made. Its genesis is to be found in the Doric, but it has come a long way from its original. The pilaster on the corner has reeds instead of flutes; and the reeds have no proper termination, they merely butt in to the neck mold, which, by the way, most of us would consider not only a poor choice of molding but out of scale as well. The cap of the pilaster does not support the architrave but returns on itself against the frieze, and the

Detail of Cornice
CONGREGATIONAL CHURCH, EAST CANAAN, CONNECTICUT

molding which acts as architrave lines up with the bottom of the cap, yet does not intersect with it, and returns on itself as does the cap. Since the architrave is much smaller than the cap, the frieze is shorter at the corners than between the pilasters. The cornice itself is not far from certain classic examples, although the mutules are undernourished, and the guttae supposedly proper to the order

one which shows a sensitive feeling for moldings, and a nice appreciation of the function of the cornice as a decorative band rather than a structural feature.

An entirely similar criticism can be made of the cornice of the Congregational Church at East Canaan, Connecticut (pg. 73). The pilaster projects too far, and the entablature above shows no

Detail of Cornice
HOUSE AT EAST MARION, LONG ISLAND

are replaced by six round holes bored in the soffit in an ornamental pattern. The turning of the corner between the rake of the gable and the horizontal, always difficult, is here most awkwardly managed; really it is not managed at all. And what shall we say of the row of dentils like drops below the bed mold? Is this part of the cornice or a decoration to the frieze? Altogether it is a most amateurish piece of work, and yet

classic articulation; architrave, frieze and cornice are jumbled together so that it is practically impossible to describe portions of it as belonging to any one of the three. The corona is lacking, the fillet below the cymatium serves as corona, and the soffit is not countersunk; but the whole composition is a sound design for the crown motive of a rather important building.

The colonial designers seem to have been quite

Angle View
GENERAL STRONG HOUSE, VERGENNES, VERMONT

strongly impressed with the value of recurring decorative motives as opposed to continuous decoration on the frieze, and we find very many cornices either with or without mutules, which have decorations on their friezes derived from the triglyph. In the example last referred to (pg. 73) the principal ornament is a series of lozenge shaped pieces of wood counter-sunk in the frieze, and separated by sets of five upright reeds; this is certainly very reminiscent of the triglyph and

about 1820. Although it does appear somewhat out of place in a cornice of such mannered proportions as those of the Vergennes house. The contrast is especially bad between the series of black and whites of the row of consoles, the lesser row of dentils and the triglyphs. The triglyphs (which should be most important) are out of scale and insignificant by reason of their small size and lack of depth. In the "King Caesar" House at Duxbury, Mass., built in 1794, (below)

Detail of Cornice
"KING CAESAR" HOUSE — 1794 — DUXBURY, MASSACHUSETTS

metope, although the spacing of the ornament bears no relation to the spacing of the mutules. In the frieze of the house at East Marion, Long Island (pg. 74) the triglyphs are represented by reeded pieces of board spaced on centers *between* the mutules; and these pseudo-triglyphs do not extend the full height of the frieze to rest on the architrave, but are pendant from the bed mold. The treatment of the frieze of the house at Vergennes, Vermont (pg. 75), is similar, but perhaps a little better done, as is natural in a house built

triglyphs are suggested by sets of three deep grooves cut in the lowest of the bed molds. This photograph shows another very characteristic and curious ornamental form which appears often in the cornices of the time: the rope ornament bed mold with auger holes bored in patterns, so that one hardly knows whether the designer intended to simulate leaves or rope. Perhaps he did not know himself, but at least he succeeded in producing a "color" of surface that is unique. The ornament is not altogether pleasant in such large

Detail of Cornice
CHURCH AT SOUTH HADLEY, MASSACHUSETTS

Detail of Cornice
HOUSE AT EAST HARTFORD, CONNECTICUT

quantities, as in the church at South Hadley, Massachusetts, (pg. 77) where it is used not only as a principal bed mold, but also as the crown mold of the Doric cap, much as leaf ornament was used by the Italian architects of the Renaissance.

The same general type of ornament is used in the house at East Hartford, Connecticut (above), but the placing of the auger holes has given this a distinctly leaf-like quality; and immediately below it we have a dentil course composed of guttae, which is not unusual at this period when the dentil course was a favorite motive and rarely used in its original form.

This concludes the list of motives to be discussed in this issue; it was originally the intention of the editor to treat the subject of ornamental cornices in a single number, but so many interesting variations of the simple motives were found, that it became necessary to continue the subject through another chapter. Part Two will discuss other ornamental motives commonly used by our early designers, as well as a further consideration of the probable sources from which they borrowed. We know far too little both of these sources and of the men who worked from them; there is no full and authentic record of the training of any American architect before Bulfinch, and what we know of him would lead us to believe that his training was far more complete than that of most of his contemporaries—a deduction borne out by the fact that his work is more classic and more mannered than that of other men of his time. Yet what he gained in knowledge he seems to have lost in freedom, for while his buildings excell other early work, both in proportion and in scale, somehow they lack the interest in detail which the less knowing carpenter-architects, who were responsible for most of the cornices shown in these illustrations, imparted to their work.

Early American Ornamental Cornices, Part Two

Text by
Aymar Embury II
Photographs by
Kenneth Clark
Originally published in 1924 as White Pine Monograph
Volume X, Number 3

Detail of Cornice
CABOT-CHURCHILL HOUSE — 1803 — BRISTOL, RHODE ISLAND
The eagles, one poised over each corner, were carved out of White Pine, according
to tradition, by sailors of the intrepid *Yankee* of which Capt. Churchill was Master.

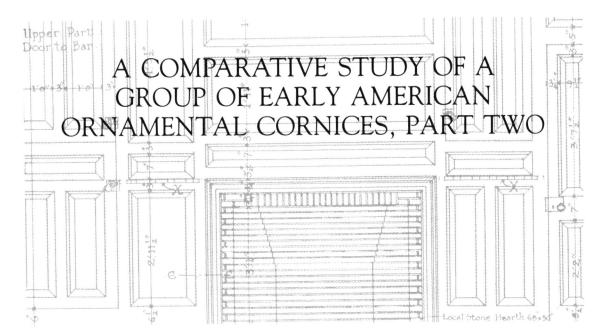

A COMPARATIVE STUDY OF A
GROUP OF EARLY AMERICAN
ORNAMENTAL CORNICES, PART TWO

IN the preceding chapter on Early American
Ornamental Cornices, were discussed the types
of design and the methods of ornament used
by our designers previous to the beginning
of the nineteenth century, not because the
year 1800 is a date easy to remember, but because at about that time there was a very marked
change in the character of the work. The Classic
Revival began to make its influence felt in the
country, and the light and graceful architecture
which we justly call "Colonial," regardless of its
date, passed out of existence, to make way for the
mannered style of the early nineteenth century.
The origin of the ornament used in the Classic
Revival work is for the most part as obvious as that
of the Colonial is obscure; the similarity of many
of the motives to the work of the Adam brothers
in England was early noted and much commented
upon; yet it seems doubtful if they had any direct
influence so early as 1790 in the country districts
of the United States, since their work had only
become popular about 1770 and from 1775 until
1783 the Revolutionary War had been fought. It
is more probable that just as the Adam work was
an expression of the quality of architectural
thought of the day, so was the corresponding work
in America. One thing we can be certain of; that
neither the work of the Adams, nor of any other
English architect, compared with the early
American in the beauty and delicacy of the run
moldings at this time. In England they continued

to use the old repertoire, cyma and cyma reversa,
ovolo and cavetto, mostly composed of arcs of
circles, while here, working in wood, our designers
produced moldings airy and graceful, often
without mathematical curves, resembling
sometimes the Gothic, sometimes the Greek, and
sometimes those of no other period, but exqui-
sitely adapted to the material, and to the free,
almost bizarre, ornament with which they were
combined.

One probable source to which the American
builder-architect resorted for motives was unquestionably furniture, either in the executed
pieces, or in the catalogs of the various English
manufactures; and with furniture must be included mantels, since these were often made by
furniture factories and illustrations of them were
included in the catalogs. There was at that time
a rather curious condition in England; furniture
design had long borrowed motives from architecture and much early furniture was designed by
architects, but during the latter half of the eighteenth century men who began their careers as
cabinet-makers became architects, and in the design of houses we find many motives obviously
borrowed from furniture design. It is likely then
that occasional American architects closely in
touch with English work, derived the new motives which suddenly appeared toward the close
of the century from English furniture books,
and it is likewise probable that the American

compilers of architectural books, men like Pain and Asher Benjamin, copied or at least freely transcribed from them. As the Adam brothers were the authors of books on furniture and architectural design, it is quite possible that they influenced American work to an extent that is not realized, by this indirect method, but the date of their publications and work, would seem to indicate that it was rather the books of earlier men that were most used and most useful.

There was another and important factor, and that was the most admirable library possessed by most colonial builders. This may have been but a single volume, and was probably never more than three or four, but such books as *Palladio Londiniensis*," Pain's *"House Carpenter"* and Benjamin's *"Country Builder's Assistant,"* do not exist today. They contained literally all that the colonial architect needed to know, and what library is there today which gives that and no more? We have too many books, so that our instinctive feeling for design is obscured or thwarted by our conflicting knowledges. The colonial architect found himself in one strong current of design, easy to swim in because he swam with the current, not across or against it, and because he was powerfully guided and supported by his books; whereas we are directed by our libraries now across and now against the stream, and alas, we not infrequently sink, weighted down by our useless information.

Too high praise cannot be given these colonial books; it is true that not all decorative motives in our early American work are direct copies of plates in them, but it is obvious that with their publication toward the end of the eighteenth century there was an immediate and enormous increase in the number of motives commonly employed, in the use of ornamented moldings and decorated friezes, and in a sort of general release from the genuine (though degraded) classic succession of moldings. It will thus be found that the most interesting of the so-called colonial houses, especially in their detail, date from the years immediately succeeding the Revolution, and before the publication of the archaeological books on Roman and Greek work, like Stuart and Revett's *"Antiquities of Athens."* Asher Benjamin and Daniel Raynerd's book, *"The American*

Builder's Companion; or, a NEW SYSTEM OF ARCHITECTURE; Particularly Adapted to The Present Style of Building in The United States of America" was published in 1806. In the preface the authors state, "Being the first who have for a great length of time published any New System of Architecture, we do not expect to escape some degree of censure. Old-fashioned workmen, who have for many years followed the footsteps of Palladio and Langley, will, no doubt, leave their old path with great reluctance . . . We do not conceive it essentially necessary to adhere exactly to any particular order, provided the proportion and harmony of the parts be carefully preserved. If, for instance in any of the cornices an ovolo should be changed for an ogee, or for a hollow, so trifling an alteration could not destroy the effect of the whole, provided it were done with any degree of judgment." A plate made from drawings by Benjamin to illustrate this book is reproduced on the page opposite.

American artisans shone by comparison with those of other countries, in that they were so free from tradition that they dared to depart from the stereotyped. Page 85 shows the cornices of the main house, the window and the porch of the Bacon House at Kent, Connecticut, built in 1810, in all of which dentil courses and consoles appear. The porch seems to have been added rather late, since the consoles have degenerated into one board set upon another, instead of the molded solid blocks of the older work, while the porch dentils are merely small oblong blocks nailed to the frieze, without intermediate pieces. The same type of dentils are used on the main cornice, the windows and the door and show how interestingly the early builders could vary a motive which had been in use so long as to seem almost impervious to change. The short portion of the frieze is most unusual and well designed for its purpose, the vertical applied members being obviously derived from the triglyph, while the half round between them may be reminiscent of the swag. The native sense of design was usually sufficiently acute to keep the artisans within the bounds of the appropriate.

The dentil course was a favorite motive, but rarely used in its original form. Sometimes it was composed of guttae as on page 86 (top), often it

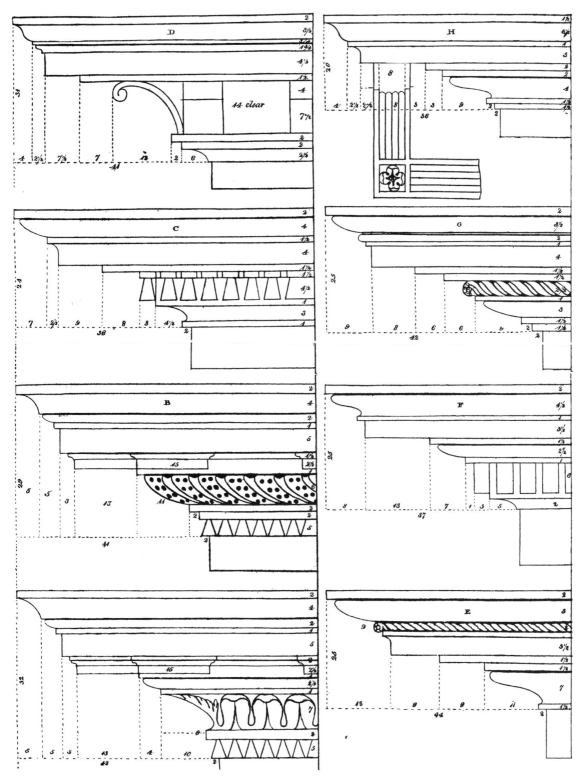

Reproduction of Plate 12 — *"The American Builder's Companion"*
By Asher Benjamin. Published at Boston in 1806.

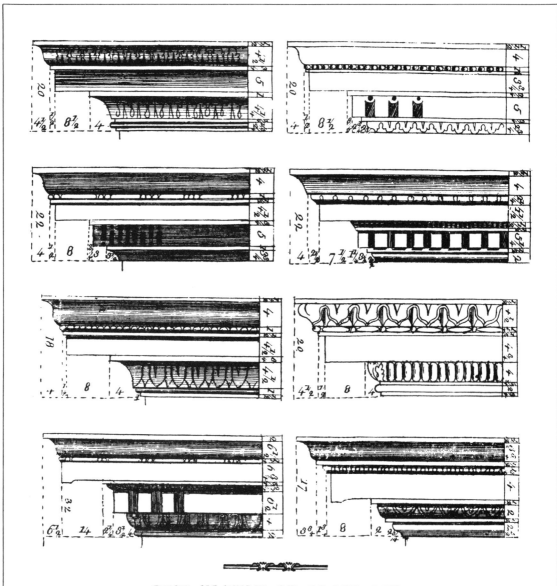

EXPLANATION OF PLATE LIV.

TO proportion the cornice and frize to rooms, or any place required ; give them three fourths of an inch to a foot, including the frize and necking ; fuppofe them to be fourteen feet, more or lefs ; at fourteen feet the cornice and frize, including the necking, will be 10½ inches ; divide that into 12 parts, give 5 to the cornice, 6 to the frize, and one to the necking ; if cornices are ufed without frize or necking, give them three eighths of an inch to a foot, or half an inch to a foot ; fuppofe 14 feet as before, at three eighths of an inch to a foot, the cornice will be 5¼ inches : at half an inch to the foot, the cornice will be 7 inches ; whatever the given height is, that muft be divided into the fame number of parts as the cornice you make ufe of, and difpofe them to the parts in height and projection, as figured on the cornices.

Reproductions of Plates and Text from
PAIN'S "PRACTICAL HOUSE CARPENTER"

became a combination of the Greek fret and the dentil as shown on pages 80, 86 (bottom) and 89, and sometimes a row of drops either turned or square, as below and page 87 (top).

Another frequently used motive in early American cornices is one for which there is no name, or at least no name in common use; the curious row of curved corbels seen on pages 80 and 87. The origin of this motive is doubtful; a full cove furniture before 1800; so that it was most likely a transformed furniture design used in architecture. The motive was published here before 1800 and very likely in England also, so that by 1799 when the Pierce House at Portsmouth, New Hampshire (pg. 87), was built it was an accepted part of the architect's repertory. This house, by the way, is attributed to Bulfinch, and while the writer has no facts to support this attribution, the

Detail of Cornice
BACON HOUSE — 1810 — KENT, CONNECTICUT

used as a cornice was not uncommon in colonial times; some of the earliest wood buildings in Massachusetts had plaster coves of this shape below the corona, and it remained a common crown motive on the brick and stone buildings around Philadelphia. It has been asserted that the curved consol was derived from the cove cornice. This seems hardly likely in view of the fact that while the motive was not common in England it was by no means unknown, and is frequently found in house itself by its correct and mannered design is evidence that it was not the off-hand product of some local carpenter-architect, even in a place where the average work was of so excellent a quality.

It is an old adage that the best work has in it something of imperfection, and this is again demonstrated by a comparison with the Pierce House and the Cabot-Churchill House at Bristol, Rhode Island (pg. 80). The latter, built in 1803,

Detail of Cornice
OLD PARKER HOUSE — 1790 — ESSEX, CONNECTICUT

Detail of Entrance Cornice
PRUDENCE CRANDALL HOUSE — 1800 — CANTERBURY, CONNECTICUT

Detail of Cornice
JOHN PIERCE HOUSE — 1799 — PORTSMOUTH, NEW HAMPSHIRE

Detail of Cornice — Front Door
CHASE HOUSE, NEWBURYPORT, MASSACHUSETTS

four years after the Pierce House, is far less sophisticated and yet more interesting. One can hardly uphold the railing as a model for copyists, the cymatium is probably too big and the dentil course too small to be perfect in scale, yet the whole cornice possesses a vigorous and insistent individuality rarely found in technically more skillful work. The eagles at the four corners doubtless aid in producing this sen-

ornament simulating swags. The drops are tapered turned wood pegs nailed to the frieze, with the swags between carved in arcs of a circle; there is no indication of cloth, or of any other material, and yet the general effect is very pleasant, especially as emphasized in the photograph by the excellent leader head. This cornice has practically no soffit, the tight bead ornament below the corona being almost flush with the house, one of

Detail of Cornice
HOUSE AT SHARON, CONNECTICUT

sation, although they are by no means entirely responsible, even with the pretty legend recited in the caption.

In the last group of houses executed before the Classic Revival superseded the genuine American expression of the Renaissance, we find some very interesting treatments of the frieze below the cornices. The house at Sharon, Connecticut (above), is of the simple type with applied wood

the few examples of this kind in the country. The designer of the house at 409 Hope Street, Bristol, Rhode Island (pg. 89), "bit off more than he could chew," when he applied such a mouthful of architecture to the cornice; and his failure to appreciate the necessity of proper scale is the cause of the general bad effect of a cornice which contains some interesting features, notably the swags, and the saw tooth ornament at the bottom of the frieze. This saw tooth ornament is quite often found in furniture, especially on the frames of dressers and cupboards, but is exceedingly rare as an architectural ornament; the only other cases where it was used that come to mind being in an exterior doorway in Alexandria, Virginia, and in an interior doorway in Winchester in the Shenandoah Valley.

The house at Chatham Center, New York,

find doorways, window heads and mantels decorated and sometimes over decorated with carved sunbursts, rosettes and flutes all executed with a gouge. In the example illustrated even the urn between the sun rays could readily be cut with a gouge by a carpenter who was in no sense a carver, if he had a good layout of the design on his board.

Another furniture motive is the Chinese Chippendale interlaced fret on the frieze of the Wain-

Detail of Cornice
HOUSE AT 409 HOPE STREET, BRISTOL, RHODE ISLAND

built in 1789 (pg. 90) has a frieze ornament borrowed from plaster work, and which, though used in a curious way in this case, was quite a common method of ornamentation around New York City, especially by the workmen of Dutch descent. It was executed by a gouge only, and complicated as it appears, could be carved rapidly and cheaply by a good mechanic (he did not need to be a good carver), so that on many of the Dutch houses we

wright House at Middlebury, Vermont, built in 1807 (pg. 91). This was probably cut out with a key-hole saw and applied within a panel; and is especially satisfactory in combination with finely detailed cornice and pilasters, and the St. Andrews cross of the railing.

In the house at Nichols, Tioga County, New York (pg. 92), on a road running along the banks of the Susquehanna River (part of the old trail from the Hudson at Kingston to the headwaters of the Delaware at Unadilla), the decoration of the frieze has really a functional part to play in the design of the façade, in a manner which would make Vignola squirm, but which somehow does not seem at all forced in reality. This is a house of quite late design, with a mantel-like window trim, and though the treatment of the building is very free, it was evidently done by a man who

has perhaps little conscious attempt at personal design, and its variance from book Greek architecture is most likely due to the inability of its builder to read plans, but the "White House" at Charlestown, New Hampshire (pg. 93), is of a different sort. The classic motives appear to have been pretty clearly understood and consciously altered, not out of caprice, but from a realization that the type of triglyph and mutule,

Detail of Cornice
HOUSE AT CHATHAM CENTER, NEW YORK

knew very thoroughly what he was about. By the time this house was built, the American carpenter-architect had learned his business.

Even when what we have agreed to call the Colonial style was finally extinguished by the Greek Revival, the indigenous quality managed to make itself felt through the veneer of Greek forms. The cornice of the Windham Bank at Windham, Connecticut, built in 1832 (pg. 94)

which was suited to a marble structure with walls three feet thick, might not be appropriate to a wooden house with six-inch walls. Thus in the frieze of the "White House," we have triglyphs of lace-like delicacy and moldings of very small scale, although the classic proportion is pretty closely held.

Before this (at least to the writer) fascinating subject is laid aside a word should be said about the treatment of the gable end. Of course, in many cases, the classic theory of carrying the full cornice up the rake was adhered to, with various degrees of success at the critical point where the raking cornice intersects with the horizontal; but in a much larger number of cases the whole cornice was carried across the front only, with the corona and cymatium returning flush with the gables and the bed molds returning on

cases where he felt that a horizontal line at the cornice height was needed across the gable end, and that a full cornice was too heavy. This he solved in a number of ways, of which perhaps the most interesting was to return the main cornice on itself around the corner of the gable, but with a reduced projection, and carry the bed molds like a band across the gable; a very ingenious and sometimes lovely piece of design.

Detail of Cornice
WAINWRIGHT HOUSE — 1807 — MIDDLEBURY, VERMONT

themselves. In general, it may be said that with slopes of less than 30° the classic method appears to be the better, but for the steep roofs so common in our early work, the flat return is far the best, and in our modern houses of colonial precedent, a repeated error is to return the horizontal cornice across the gable end on all shapes of roof, making a true pediment of bad proportion. Like ourselves, the colonial designer sometimes found

The return of the main cornice on the gable end was always a problem, and the bad solutions we find on most present-day houses not designed by capable architects (and even on some which are), indicate better than words the ability in design of the old craftsmen, although the actual execution often fell behind the conception. As has just been said, the return of the full cornice at normal projection across the gables is the exception rather than the rule; the most usual solution was to terminate the cornice somewhere near the corner, between the front and the gable end, finishing the gable end with a rake mold, but the exact point of termination was not fixed by custom. We find many cases where the full cornice was returned for a short distance around the corner, a distance only determined by what the designer considered appropriate unless corner pilas-

molds, frieze and architrave returned upon themselves on the front of the building, perhaps with the inside edge of the corner board as a limiting point.

All the above treatments give a shelf upon which the end of the rake molds or verge boards may rest, but there are also many instances where the complete cornice extends as a decorative bank on the front only, returned upon itself

Detail of Cornice
HOUSE AT NICHOLS, TIOGA COUNTY, NEW YORK

ters were used, in which case the edge of the pilaster was naturally the limiting element; we find other cases in which all members of the cornice are returned but with a soffit greatly reduced in width so that the cornice becomes a sort of fragment of the belt course at each corner of the gable end; and perhaps the happiest solution is that in which only the corona and cymatium are returned around the corner with all bed

as close as possible to the corner, but not around it. This left the rake mold (invariably present), to take care of itself at the bottom; a very awkward thing to manage and one which the colonial architects found too much for them. Sometimes the foot of the rake was cut to the profile of the corona and cymatium and these members butted against it, sometimes the verge board turned at an angle and became the corner board

Detail of Cornice and Pilaster
"THE WHITE HOUSE," CHARLESTOWN, NEW HAMPSHIRE

with the small mold at its top, below the over-hanging shingles left in the air at the bottom, and sometimes the two returned around the corner at the front to meet the cornice. This was, of course, possible only with a box gutter and when the slope of the roof intersected the wall line at or near the height of the top of the cornice itself. Some of these methods were only partially successful, but it is undoubtedly true that even the poorest was better than a direct copy of the Classic cornice applied to the wood-built country house.

The illustrations in these chapters should be sufficient to prove to the American architect how great a scope even a limited field offers to a man of ideas and imagination. In our present struggle for originality we tend to look to exotic architectures and bizarre motives for precedents, and by copying these things we seek for something new, regardless of its appropriateness to our civilization or our methods of construction. The colonial architect knew less than we, and perhaps in that was his salvation, for he was forced by his own limitations to express himself within them to the everlasting advantage of his art.

Detail of Cornice
WINDHAM BANK, WINDHAM, CONNECTICUT

Early American Exterior Windows

Text by
Aymar Embury II
Photographs by
Kenneth Clark
Originally published in 1930 as White Pine Monograph
Volume XVI, Number 2

JESSUP HOUSE, WESTPORT, CONNECTICUT

A COMPARATIVE STUDY OF A GROUP OF EARLY AMERICAN WINDOWS

ORNAMENTAL features in the early American house were confined to salient points, especially the doors, usually the cornices, and to a less degree the windows. Windows naturally need a somewhat slighter degree of decoration than do the doorways; in the first place it is not necessary to mark them for identification as it were, and in the second place, the patterns of the muntins dividing the panes in themselves are an agreeable ornamental feature when their proportion is correct as compared with the sizes of the openings and the mass of the building in which these openings are pierced. It has however been an architectural habit since very early times, and in practically all styles, to introduce some form of decoration in and around the windows. In Gothic architecture, of course, it was the divisions between the windows which became of importance, to the neglect of the wall surrounding them; in the Renaissance period it was the frame of the window that was of importance rather than the window itself, and since our colonial architecture was derived from that of the Renaissance this decorative treatment of the frame of the opening rather than of the divisions of the openings was the one employed when any ornament at all was thought to be necessary. There are of course exceptions to this; circular headed windows very frequently had interesting tracery motifs used in the divisions of the sash into lights, and transom lights and side lights of doors or triple windows and the circular or semi-circular or elliptical windows in the gable ends were often amusingly divided, so often in fact that certain methods of division came to be commonly accepted stock motifs, as for example the "globe" window in the gable ends.

These were however especial cases and for the most part the colonial architects contented themselves with plain rectangular openings divided into smaller rectangles and decorated, where decoration was attempted, by an ornamental hood, without any change in the architraves of the jambs of the windows and at the sill. In very many of the simpler houses (though not necessarily the smaller ones) no special decorative treatment was attempted and it was rarely that in country houses of stone or brick that any treatment of the hoods or bottoms of the windows for purely decorative purposes was introduced. In these masonry structures the lintel was less common than the flat or segmental arch, sometimes with stone key blocks and occasionally with a plain brick key block as on page 100; in stone houses brick arches were very frequently used to support the walls above, the centering of these arches being a heavy oak beam left in place. Such examples are shown on pages 100 and 101, the lion's head key block in the Van Courtlandt House being the only one known to the writer in America. For the most part, however, the earlier houses were of wood and the windows were framed with a simple architrave, either molded or plain with a hood extending across the head and returning upon itself at the ends. This hood was in practically all cases derived from the classic cornice, sometimes being only the cymatium as on page 102, sometimes the full cornice as on page 116, and sometimes a frieze and cornice which together with the architrave gives a full entablature as on page 112. Once in a while the window was treated with a motive derived from the full order as on page 113, although in the Bacon House at Kent, Connecticut, the pilasters at the side are indicated only.

Since practically all Colonial houses have blinds or shutters on the exterior, the treatment of the architraves or jambs was obviously of little importance. The blinds when open covered this portion of the window completely and as a matter of fact a pilaster would have been a nuisance rather than a help because of its interference with the swing of the blind unless reduced to a very flat projection. The heads were usually horizontal and the great variety of interesting treatments which our colonial ancestors discovered for this simple feature is remarkable unless we remember the extreme freedom with which they varied traditional cornice forms and consider that the heads of the windows are after all cornices in miniature. Take for example the Bacon House (page 112) and the Strong House (page 113). In the Strong House, a triglyph is suggested by the application of half-round molding of various lengths with the ends cut off, while in the Bacon House we have a sort of dentil course running half way down the frieze and the corona and the cymatium of the cornice broken and covered in an amusing and picturesque manner, unprecedented in Renaissance work although obviously suggested by the breaks of the cornices over the columns or pilasters in certain forms of Renaissance wall treatment. These architects did not, however, stop at horizontal hoods; pediments, broken pediments, and scroll pediments, were familiar to them as on pages 114 and 115, those in the Wolcott House at Litchfield,

Connecticut, and the Pepperill House Saco, Maine, approaching the classic form very closely, while the broken pediment of the Moulton House at Hampton, New Hampshire, could only exist in the early architecture of the United States although its genesis is clearly to be seen. We have here an approximation to the classic scroll pediment with a pineapple in the center so familiar in Georgian work, but here with the scrolls meeting and the pineapple (translated into an acorn) hung from a point in the junction of the scrolls rather than standing upright between them.

Our architects however were by no means limited to a single motive. In the Vernon House (pages 110 and 111) the walls of which are of wood carved to imitate stone, the head was fashioned in a manner reminiscent of the flat stone arch and in The Old Manse at Suffield, Connecticut (pages 118 and 119), a sort of double key block of wood is inserted in the middle of the head trim, a variation of wooden architecture obviously derived from stone, and in the Jessup House (page 96 and page 109) a rather late example, we have a combination of the pilaster trim with panel backs and a flat head trim surmounted by an arch form consisting merely of a molding with flush boards in the semicircle to distinguish it from the shingle walls of the building. In the Ruggles House at Columbia Falls, Maine, the walls are entirely of flush boards with sawn wood pieces applied to these boards in imitation of the familiar cloth swags of Empire design.

The treatment of the heads of the windows has however very little effect upon the appearance of the house as a whole unless they project so far as to cast very large and distinct shadows. An observant architect may have often passed a Colonial house which he admires extremely without noticing the treatment of the heads of the windows at all, and this because the pattern of the muntins against the dark of the window is so much more strongly marked than the lighter and more delicate shadows cast by the window heads; and it is likely that in most of our modern imitations of Colonial work the failure to reproduce the Colonial characteristics arises more often from a bad division of the window opening than from any other cause except a fundamental un-Colonial mass form of the building. There is also a very real and important connection in Colonial between the division of the openings and the shape of the structure in which they occur; whether this is because we are accustomed to seeing certain types of sash correspond to houses of certain shapes, or whether it is because there is a positive relation between the two is difficult to say. It is however certain that the early houses were of a different mass than the later ones, that

the lights of glass were smaller and that the muntins were heavier. It has often been stated (probably with truth) that the shapes of the old windows were determined by the sizes of the glass available. We know that large panes were impossible to obtain in the colonies before the beginning of the seventeenth century and very difficult to obtain until about the time of the Revolutionary war. Likewise the later craftsmen discovered better practices of woodworking, and endeavoring to keep the muntins to a minimum width, reduced them to sizes which are difficult for our mills to follow today. The early muntins averaged perhaps an inch in width whereas the later ones rarely exceed five-eights of an inch and were occasionally as thin as one-half an inch so that the earlier windows, as for example that shown on page 102, had a feeling of strength and solidity compared with an almost spider web lightness of the muntins in the house at Waldens Bridge, New York, illustrated on page 112. It must not be assumed that there was any sharp division of practice at any given date, the sections of the country were at that time far more separated than is today the case and the practice of any craftsmanship was dependent upon the tradition of the neighborhood to an extent that will never again be the case. It was about at the middle of the eighteenth century that in the large centers of population a very decided change in the quality of craftsmanship was taking place, while in the remoter parts of the country the earlier practices were still obtained; we have for example in the little town of Clinton, Georgia, and in the outskirts of Chilicothe, Ohio, houses which should be dated 1750 instead of 1820 so far as their methods of design and of construction go. The Colonial tradition still lived in these remote districts when the Greek Revival had overwhelmed the older style in New York and Boston.

It is a remarkable thing that this Colonial architecture of ours so limited in its materials, so hampered by the great cost of labor as compared with wealth of the day, produced so many and such interesting variances from tradition. It may indeed have been that the factors which we assume to have been hampering ones were actually those which produced its quality. Conklin, the biologist, in his discussion of heredity and environment, says that in our struggle to improve the environment of the American people we have forgotten that we do not know what is the proper environment. Lincoln, for example, born to a life of ease, would certainly not have been the Lincoln he was, and it is certainly possible or indeed most probable that given a "better environment" he would have been a less useful man. So with our architecture.

KNEELAND HOUSE, HARTFORD, VERMONT

VAN COURTLANDT MANSION, NEW YORK, NEW YORK

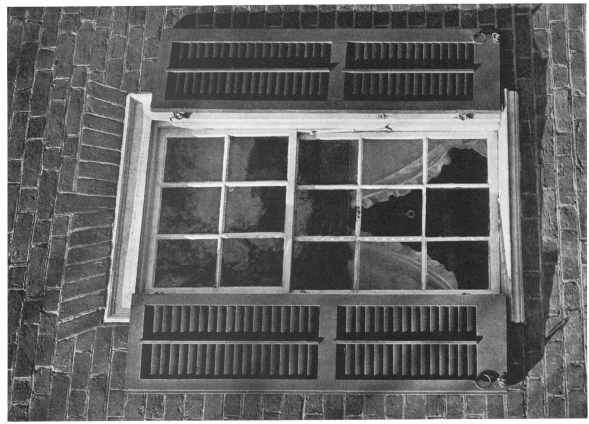

JOHN VOGLER HOUSE, WINSTON-SALEM, NORTH CAROLINA

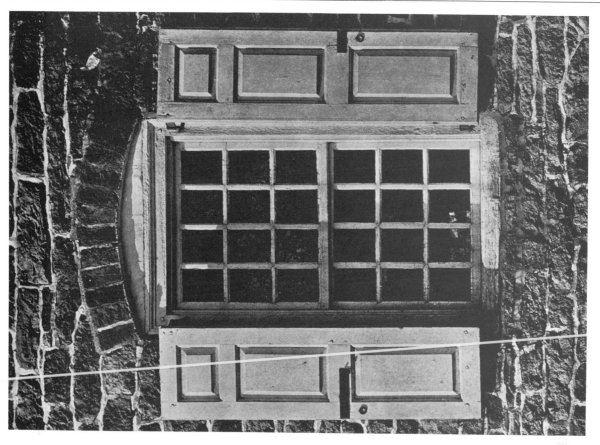

MEETING HOUSE NEAR HOPEWELL, BUCKS COUNTY, PA.

BELL HOUSE, MORAVIAN SEMINARY, BETHLEHEM, PA.

JUDGE LEE HOUSE, CAMBRIDGE, MASSACHUSETTS

GENERAL REED HOUSE, FITZWILLIAM, NEW HAMPSHIRE

LEE-SMITH HOUSE, WISCASSET, MAINE

FAIRFAX HOUSE, CAMERON STREET, ALEXANDRIA, VIRGINIA

MASONIC LODGE ROOM, NEW BERN, NORTH CAROLINA

Interior Elevation of Living Room Window
JAMES BRICE HOUSE, ANNAPOLIS, MARYLAND

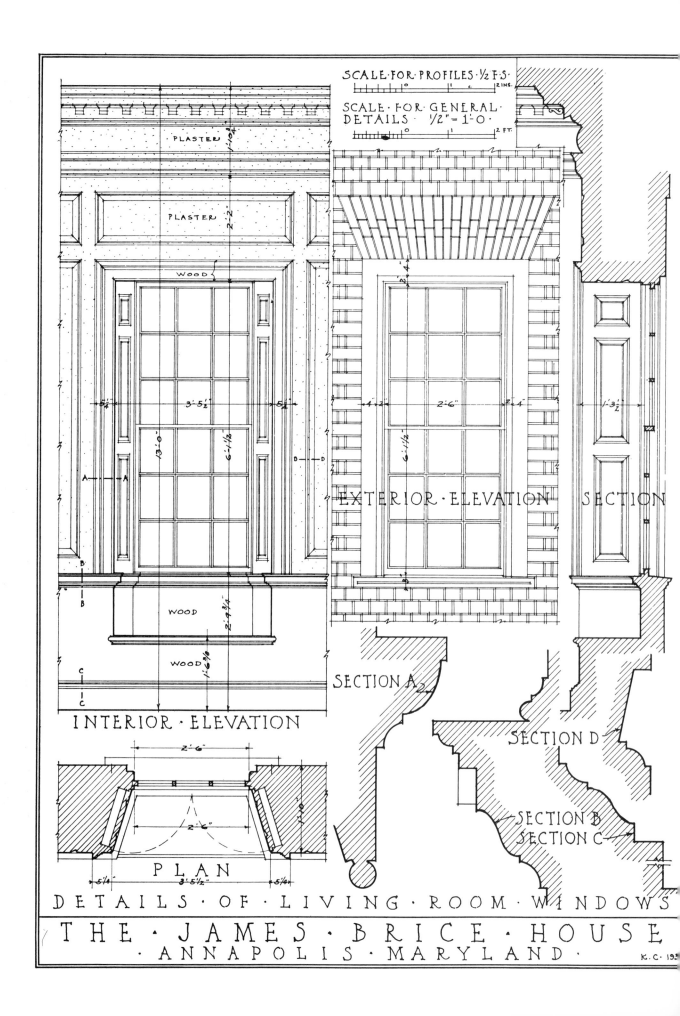

SCALE·FOR·PROFILES·½ F·S·

SCALE·FOR·GENERAL·
DETAILS· ½"=1'-0

PLASTER

PLASTER

WOOD

WOOD

WOOD

WOOD

INTERIOR·ELEVATION

EXTERIOR·ELEVATION   SECTION

SECTION A

SECTION D

SECTION B
SECTION C

PLAN

DETAILS·OF·LIVING·ROOM·WINDOWS

THE·JAMES·BRICE·HOUSE
·ANNAPOLIS·MARYLAND·

K.C.·193

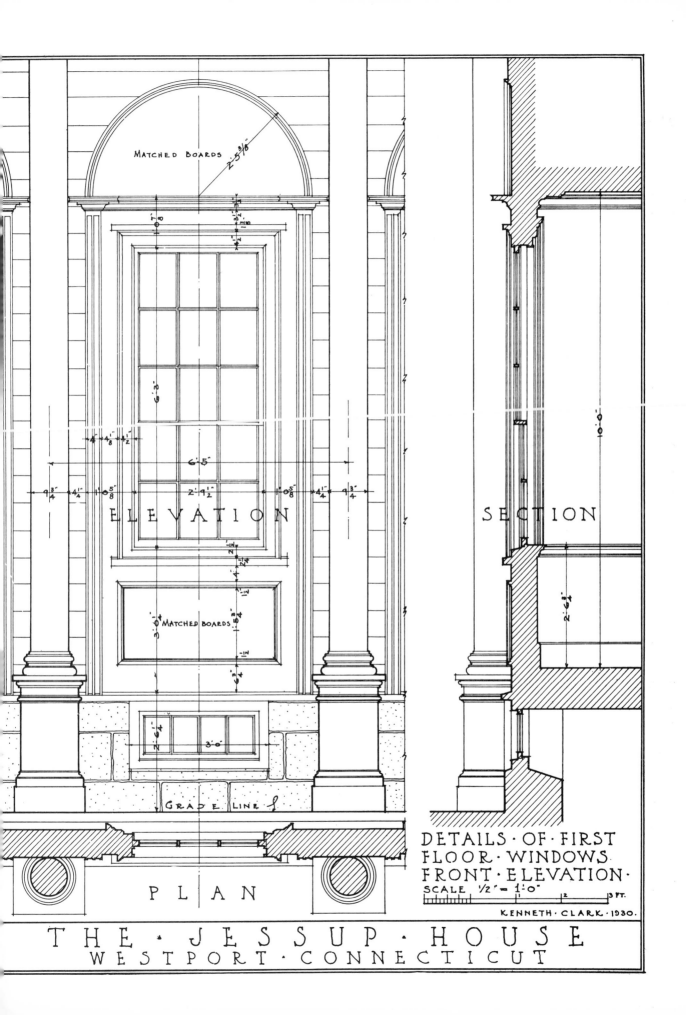

MATCHED BOARDS

ELEVATION

SECTION

MATCHED BOARDS

GRADE LINE

PLAN

DETAILS · OF · FIRST
FLOOR · WINDOWS
FRONT · ELEVATION
SCALE 1/2' = 1'-0"

KENNETH · CLARK · 1930.

THE · JESSUP · HOUSE
WESTPORT · CONNECTICUT

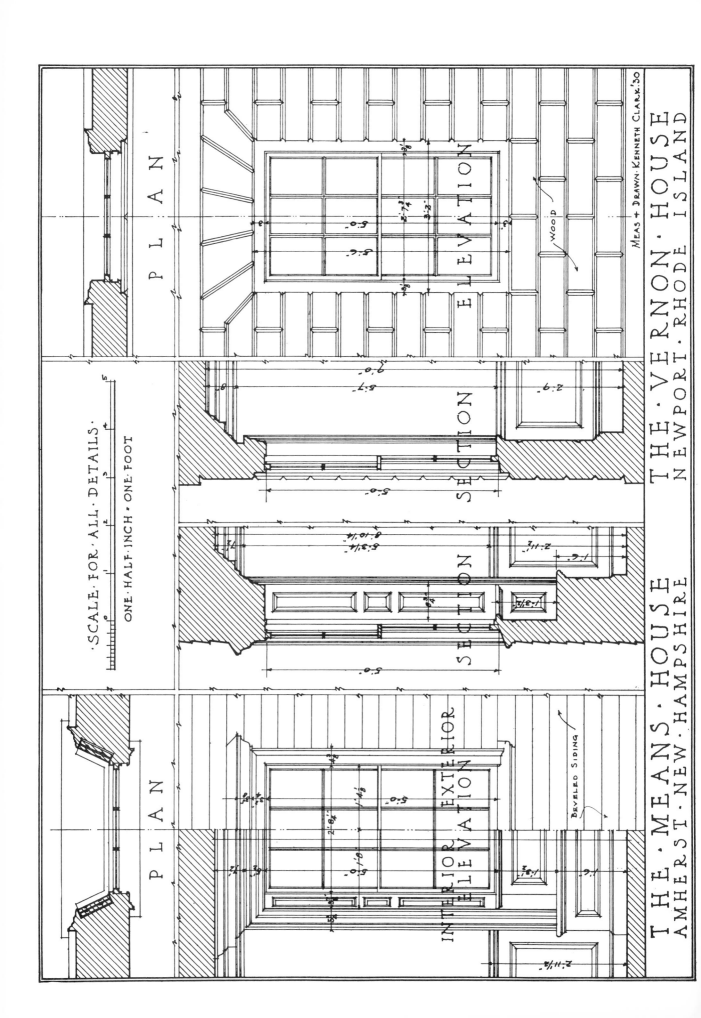

P L A N

E L E V A T I O N

WOOD

S E C T I O N

S E C T I O N

·SCALE·FOR·ALL·DETAILS·

ONE·HALF·INCH·ONE·FOOT

P L A N

INTERIOR EXTERIOR
ELEVATION

BEVELED SIDING

MEAS·+·DRAWN·KENNETH·CLARK·'30

THE·VERNON·HOUSE
NEWPORT·RHODE·ISLAND

THE·MEANS·HOUSE
AMHERST·NEW·HAMPSHIRE

VERNON HOUSE, NEWPORT, RHODE ISLAND

COL. ROBERT MEANS HOUSE, AMHERST, NEW HAMPSHIRE

BACON HOUSE, KENT, CONNECTICUT

HOUSE AT WALDENS BRIDGE, NEW YORK

GEN. STRONG HOUSE, VERGENNES, VERMONT

HOUSE AT EAST HARTFORD, CONNECTICUT

PEPPERELL HOUSE, SACO, MAINE

GEN. MOULTON HOUSE, HAMPTON, NEW HAMPSHIRE

WOLCOTT HOUSE, LITCHFIELD, CONNECTICUT

WARHAM WILLIAMS HOUSE, NORTHFORD, CONNECTICUT

"THE SYCAMORES," SOUTH HADLEY, MASSACHUSETTS

FIELD HOUSE, LONGMEADOW, MASSACHUSETTS

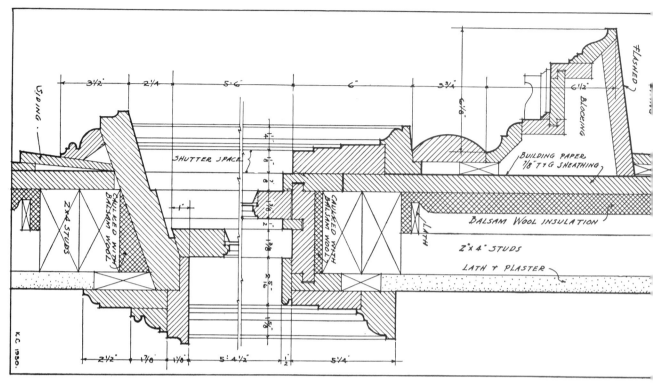

CONSTRUCTION DETAILS OF A WINDOW AT THE FIELD HOUSE,
LONGMEADOW, MASSACHUSETTS

THE OLD MANSE — 1742 — SUFFIELD, CONNECTICUT

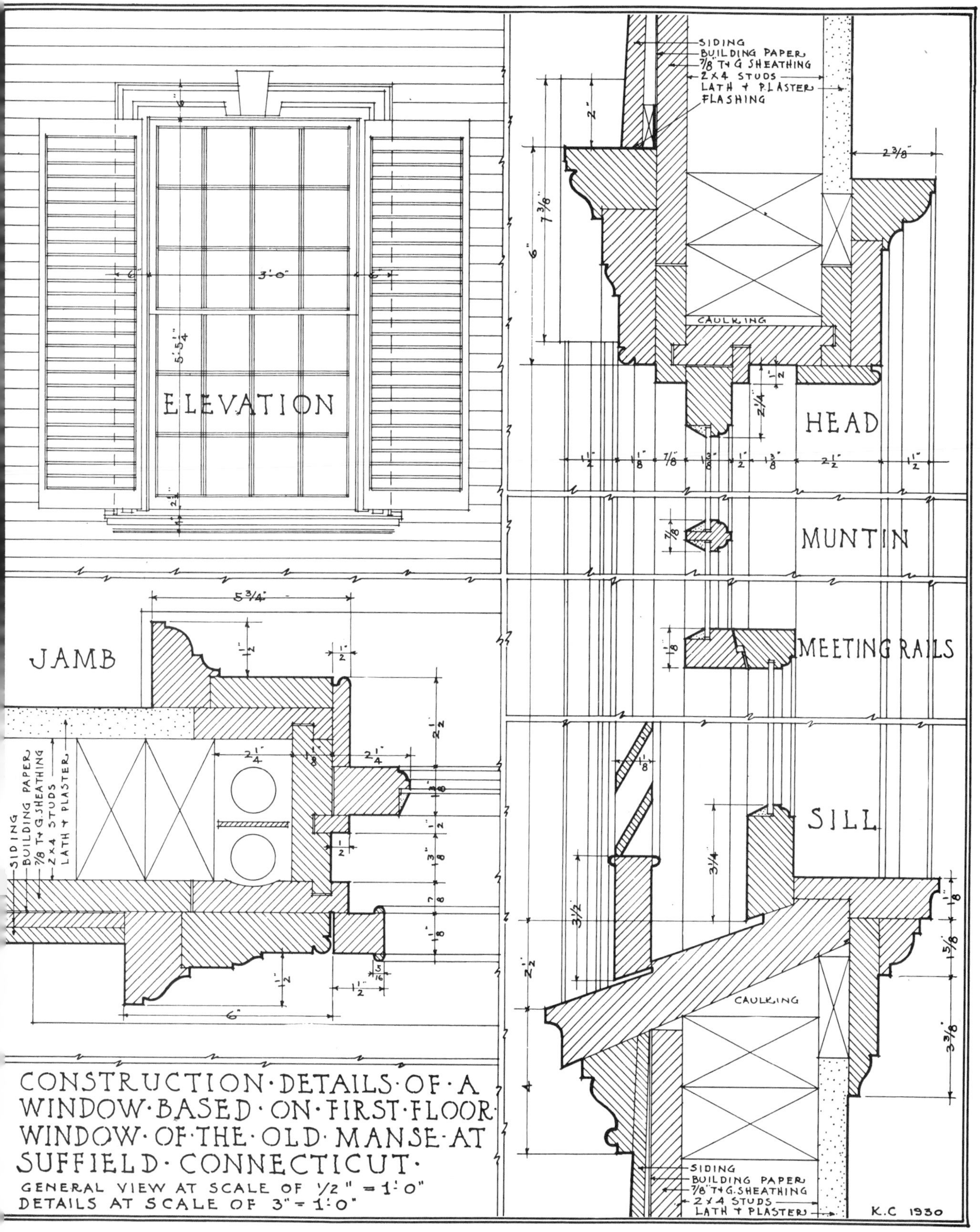
ELEVATION
6"
3'-0"
6"
5'-5 1/4"
2"
2"
JAMB
5 3/4"
1/2"
1/2"
2 1/2"
2 1/4"
1 1/8"
2 1/4"
1 3/8"
1/2"
1/2"
3/8"
7/8"
1 1/8"
1/2"
5/16
1 1/2"
6"
SIDING
BUILDING PAPER
7/8 T+G. SHEATHING
2x4 STUDS
LATH + PLASTER
SIDING
BUILDING PAPER
7/8" T+G SHEATHING
2x4 STUDS
LATH + PLASTER
FLASHING
2"
7 3/8"
6"
2 3/8"
CAULKING
1/2"
2 1/4"
HEAD
1 1/2"
1 1/8"
7/8"
1 3/8"
1/2"
1 3/8"
2 1/2"
1 1/2"
MUNTIN
7/8
MEETING RAILS
1 1/8
1 1/8"
SILL
3 1/4
3 1/2
2 1/2
4
1 1/8
1 5/8
3 3/8
CAULKING
SIDING
BUILDING PAPER
7/8" T+G. SHEATHING
2x4 STUDS
LATH + PLASTER
K.C 1930

CONSTRUCTION·DETAILS·OF·A WINDOW·BASED·ON·FIRST·FLOOR WINDOW·OF·THE·OLD·MANSE·AT SUFFIELD·CONNECTICUT·

GENERAL VIEW AT SCALE OF 1/2" = 1'-0"
DETAILS AT SCALE OF 3" = 1'-0"

HOUSE AT NORWICH, VERMONT

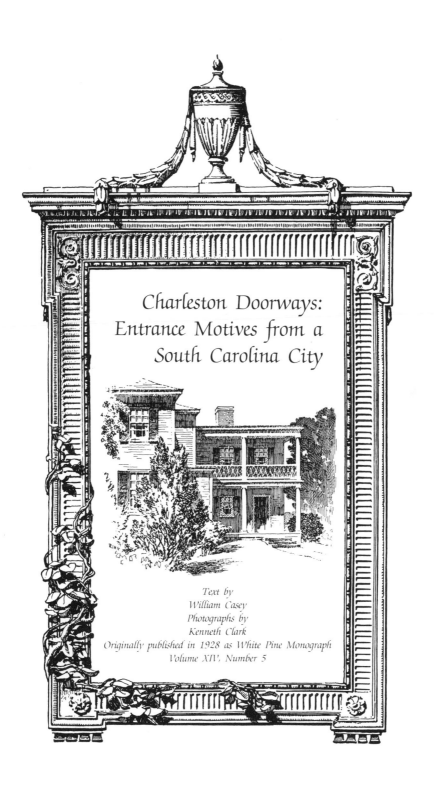

Charleston Doorways:
Entrance Motives from a
South Carolina City

Text by
William Casey
Photographs by
Kenneth Clark
Originally published in 1928 as White Pine Monograph
Volume XIV, Number 5

Entrance
SAINT ANDREW'S EPISCOPAL CHURCH — 1706 — CHARLESTON, SOUTH CAROLINA

CHARLESTON DOORWAYS: ENTRANCE MOTIVES FROM A SOUTH CAROLINA CITY

THOUGH architecture is unquestionably the most "human" of all the arts, it is less understood by the layman and the public generally than either music, painting or literature. This is perhaps because the architect is restricted in his design to materials and their use in ways that make it supremely difficult to express beauty of the ordinarily recognizable variety. His beauty must be that of proportion, spacing and contrast and his picture has no direct "subject" to intrigue the mind of the beholder into romantic speculation and enthusiasm.

The part of the exterior design of the house that lends itself most easily as an appeal to popular appreciation is the doorway or "frontispiece" and on this the designer usually lavishes his greatest skill.

The doorway as a detail can give the key and accent to a façade and can reflect the spirit of the builder or the owner. It may be imbued with the characteristics of dignity, simplicity, pretentiousness, etc., that we usually associate with human beings, and thus subtly express to the passer-by what lies within—whether it be wealth or poverty, the warmth of hospitality or the chill of aloofness.

The development of our early American architecture can be traced more clearly, and with less deviation from the true path, by its doorways, than through any other detail. For in the doorway, the index of the style of the house and its period are most clearly indicated. Starting with the Jacobian influence apparent in the seventeenth century examples, and on through the Renaissance, Georgian and Greek Revival Periods, there is a distinct chronological path that can be followed by the investigator.

Charleston, South Carolina, offers some interesting examples that are in a way unique as to scheme and execution. The custom of placing the main entrance of the house at the street end of a side piazza or gallery, thus giving admission to the "Estate" with an entirely separate door leading from the porch to the interior of the house proper, has much to recommend it under the circumstances and habits of the families of Charleston who created a city of beautiful houses and gardens that are unsurpassed in our early work. The casual visitor on entering through the street door could be received on the porch out of the gaze of the passer-by and there entertained or having passed inspection could be welcomed to the hospitality of the house itself. Lucky is the person who comes within the latter category, for the privilege of enjoying Charleston hospitality is not lightly conferred, but once given is a thing to be remembered. Here perhaps the spirit of the old South has its firmest present hold, not the South of sentimental story book variety, but the true South of culture, refinement and solidity that has been engendered by years of association of one group of families in one environment who are homogenious enough to cast off influences that would corrupt their culture and tradition.

Page 138 shows a typical porch doorway treatment with a glimpse of the house doorway through the opening and with the main "living" part of the porch cut off from the entrance way by a movable shutter screen.

The oldest examples of Charleston houses, still standing, date back to about 1750, but of the earlier examples few are left. The period of her architects' greatest achievement was from about 1760 to the Revolution and her finest houses date from within this space of about sixteen years. While the type of plan and the general scheme of the larger houses are more or less similar, the exterior designs display an ingenious use of materials, knowingly arranged. Perhaps what is most apparent is the infinite variety of doorway motives which were used during both the early and later periods of Charleston's architectural growth. Many of these frontispieces undoubtedly perished in the fires and earthquakes that have taken toll of her buildings in the past, but enough remain to establish the fact that her early designers were fully competent and have left to us a heritage that cannot be ignored. Charleston is one of the most important architectural shrines in America.

Doorway
26 CHURCH STREET, CHARLESTON, SOUTH CAROLINA

Doorway
18 MEETING STREET, CHARLESTON, SOUTH CAROLINA

Detail of Doorway
18 MEETING STREET, CHARLESTON, SOUTH CAROLINA

Detail of Doorway
104 TRADD STREET, CHARLESTON, SOUTH CAROLINA

Doorway
104 TRADD STREET — c1772 — CHARLESTON, SOUTH CAROLINA
Col. John Stuart, Architect

Doorway
KING STREET, CHARLESTON, SOUTH CAROLINA

110 BROAD STREET — 1757 — CHARLESTON, SOUTH CAROLINA
Ralph Izard, Architect

Detail of Doorway
110 BROAD STREET — 1757 — CHARLESTON, SOUTH CAROLINA
Ralph Izard, Architect

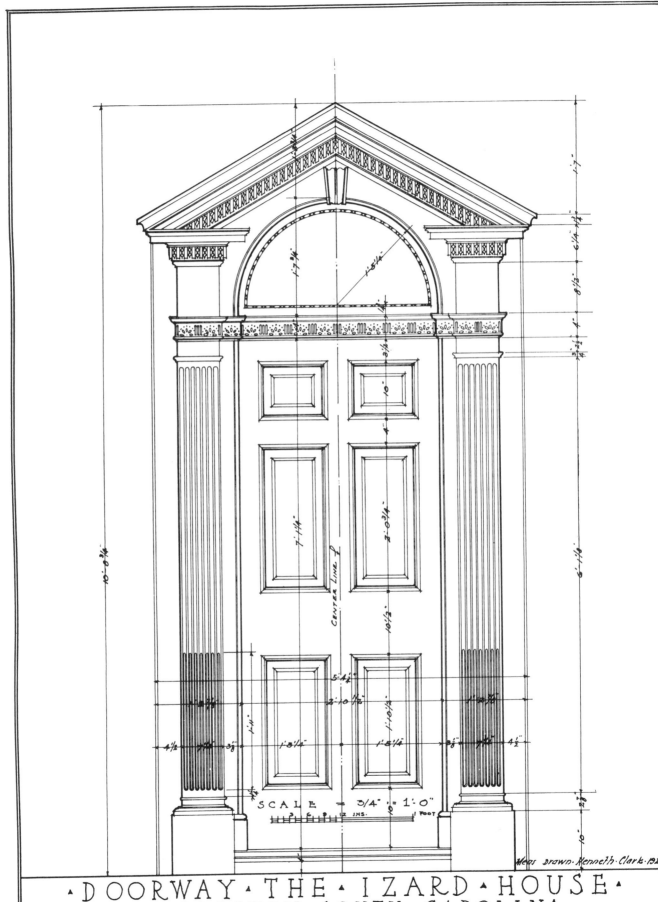

SCALE = 3/4" = 1'·0"

Meas drawn· Kenneth· Clark· 193?

·DOORWAY·THE·IZARD·HOUSE·
·CHARLESTON·SOUTH·CAROLINA·

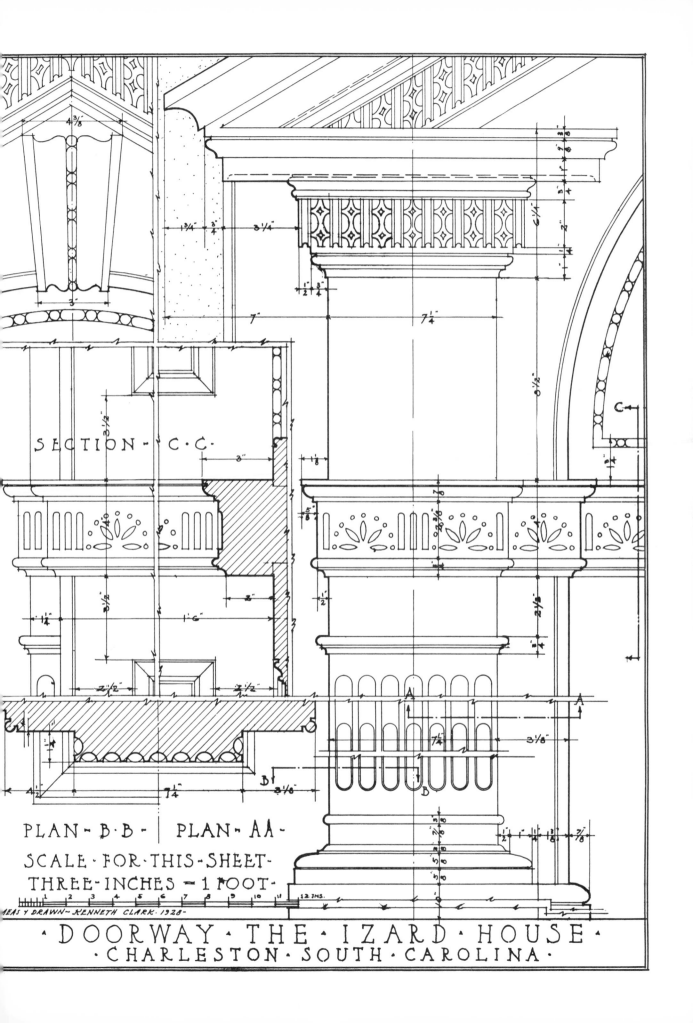

SECTION · C · C ·

PLAN · B · B · | PLAN · AA ·

SCALE · FOR · THIS · SHEET ·
THREE · INCHES = 1 · FOOT ·

MEAS'Y DRAWN~ KENNETH CLARK · 1928 ·

· DOORWAY · THE · IZARD · HOUSE ·
· CHARLESTON · SOUTH · CAROLINA ·

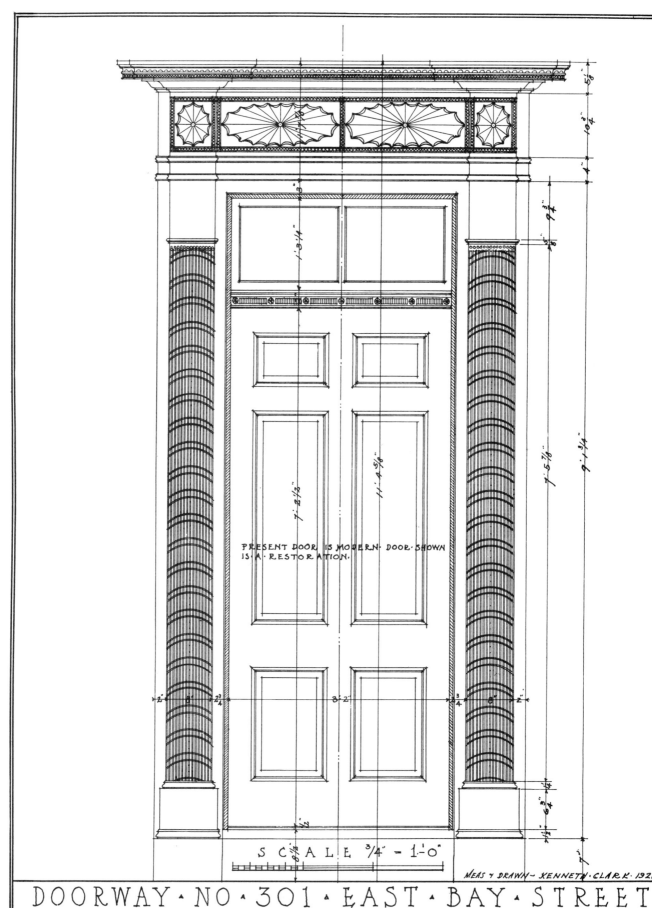

PRESENT·DOOR·IS·MODERN·DOOR·SHOWN
IS·A·RESTORATION.

SCALE ¾" = 1'-0"

MEAS·y·DRAWN~KENNETH·CLARK·1926

DOORWAY·NO·301·EAST·BAY·STREET
·CHARLESTON·SOUTH·CAROLINA·

301 EAST BAY, SOUTH, CHARLESTON, SOUTH CAROLINA

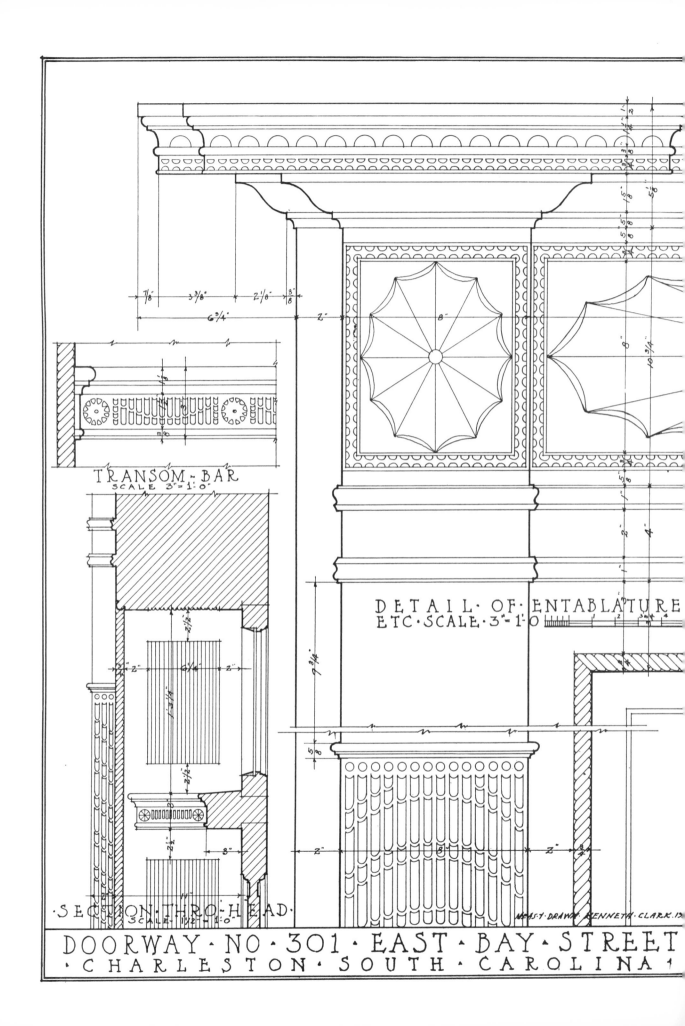

TRANSOM · BAR
SCALE 3"=1'0"

DETAIL · OF · ENTABLATURE
ETC · SCALE · 3"= 1'0"

· SECTION · THRO · HEAD ·
SCALE · 1½" = 1'0"

MEAS'T · DRAW'T · KENNETH · CLARK · 12

DOORWAY · NO · 301 · EAST · BAY · STREET
· CHARLESTON · SOUTH · CAROLINA ·

Detail of Doorway
301 EAST BAY, SOUTH, CHARLESTON, SOUTH CAROLINA

68 BROAD STREET, CHARLESTON, SOUTH CAROLINA

39 SOUTH BATTERY, CHARLESTON, SOUTH CAROLINA

Detail of Doorway
39 SOUTH BATTERY, CHARLESTON, SOUTH CAROLINA

A·DOORWAY·
BASED·ON·THE·
DOORWAY·OF·THE·
MAGWOOD·HOUSE·
AT·39·SOUTH·
BATTERY·
CHARLESTON·
SOUTH·CAROLINA

½ PLAN·A·A
SCALE 3" = 1'-0"

·PLAN·

BLOCKING

BLOCKING

GENERAL·ELEVATION
SCALE 3" = 1'-0"

·DETAIL·ELEVATION·
SCALE 3" = 1'-0"

A   A

·DRAWN·KENNETH·CLARK·1928·

SAINT JAMES CHURCH — 1711 — GOOSE CREEK, SOUTH CAROLINA

A Group of Eastern Massachusetts Vestibules

Text by
Benjamin H. Newton
Photographs by
Arthur C. Haskell
Originally published in 1934 as White Pine Monograph
Volume XX, Number 3

THE PENNIMAN-STEARNS HOUSE, BEDFORD, MASSACHUSETTS
Reuben Duren, Architect

A GROUP OF
EASTERN MASSACHUSETTS VESTIBULES

THERE is one important detail of the old Colonial house, that is rather seldom utilized by modern architects when designing a dwelling in this style—and that is the vestibule entrance, as distinct from the more conventional entrance porch. The rather late type of doorway, with side lights, under a narrow porch, is used over and over again; but the modern house designer has rather strangely overlooked the very practical projecting entrance vestibule found on many houses of early New England architecture, generally indicating a date earlier than the more open porch treatment with columns.

Yet this type of vestibule possesses a most practical means of enlarging a house plan, at precisely that point where it is often most crowded, and in the simplest and most economical way!

Probably it originally took shape from the need of meeting the demand for a larger entrance hall, with more space between entrance door and staircase. Particularly with the typical early Colonial stairway, placed against the front face of the large central chimney, the resulting passageway between the front room doors upon the first floor plan often became both narrow and crowded. When open, the door edge almost brushed the face of the stair run,—and there was little room to greet entering neighbors, particularly if they were to be welcomed within the room on that side of the house where the front door was hinged!

It was probable also that, despite the fact that the early houses were usually built with their entrance sides facing the south; this single doorway, opening directly into the front hall at the foot of the main stairs, was found to cool off the passage between the main front rooms of the house, upon both floors—especially when the house plan was changed to more nearly face the east or west; as came so frequently later to be the case.

We have also the early meeting house plan, with its one or two story vestibule—often enclosing the staircase as well—which was usually first treated as a gabled projection in its exterior handling;—until it came to be taken into the lower stories of the tower with spire, that came into general use at about the period of the building of the "Old North," or Christ Church of Boston, shown in Volume IX, Chapter 9. Here this distinctive "vestibule" type of entrance treatment had already taken a definitive form of expression—as is indicated by the original brick side vestibule upon the Old South Meeting House, on Washington Street, in that same city.

And so it was an easy step to widen the passageway across the front of the entrance hall, by taking out the front wall between the two posts that always supported the heavy timbers that framed the central chimney, and moving the doorway and wall forward some three to four feet, then filling in the two sides back to the main wall face of the house, and roofing it over either with a ridge roof forming a pediment gable upon the vestibule face, or with a simple hip roof treatment, the latter being often more appropriate to the older and simpler type of early house design.

In a large majority of instances, these entrance house vestibules were a later addition or alteration made to an older house plan. It is very rarely indeed that it can be indisputably proved that this sort of vestibule was original to the Colonial plan! Usually it is obviously a later afterthought, added to the plan to make it more habitable for the occupants during the colder seasons of the year. And it was almost always added to secure additional needed space within the hall itself. It was very rarely filled with inside coat closets; that is, in the older house plan!

In the Bedford House, indeed, the two-story vestibule shown upon the side of the house (page 144) was added apparently for the purpose of securing a small, narrow staircase from the side door to the upper story; which stairway mounts steeply along the rear or righthand side of the vestibule, over small first floor closets, to the floor above. But this is an exceptional example, with a very rarely used two-story height for this feature, found in a rather late house plan.

The one factor of the outer vestibule that often deceives the casual observer is the entrance doorway, which is generally very obviously old. And it often does not occur to one to think how easily the old doorway (and in fact, whole front wall of the hall-

25 FLINT STREET
SALEM, MASSACHUSETTS

exterior face of the original house sill, and the plates and rafters are clearly placed against the upper part of the exterior wall face, — often without even removing the clapboards or wall boarding. In these cases there can be no doubt. In the old Dillaway-Thomas House in Roxbury, for instance, built in 1750–52, the side entrance vestibule was added later, probably in 1832, when other changes were known to have been made in the dwelling at the time that it came first into the possession of the Dillaway family.

This supplies a good average date for the change or addition of this outer vestibule to be made. Many houses apparently have experienced this change from some time between 1805–10 and 1830–40. It appears then to have been a current fashion in modernization, that came into vogue at about that time, — just a little before the craze for marble Italian mantels which caused them to be imported in such large numbers, and substituted for the earlier and more delicate wooden mantels that had preceded them.

It may be stated that most outside entrance vestibules now to be found on early Colonial houses are of later date than the structures themselves; and this date of change is often extremely difficult to find. It would be best to understand that the dates given under

way, between the two upright posts) could be cut out and moved forward, to secure the wider hallway, — and that exactly in the single space where this enlargement of the plan was alone desired; — and where it could be easily secured, without causing the slightest change in anything in the rest of the house.

Sometimes the line where the old plaster was joined to the new wall on the inside of the side walls, shows up very distinctly. Sometimes it is entirely lost because of the manner in which the new side walls of the vestibule are finished around and up to the two main house wall posts that are found placed in these locations. Occasionally, in houses built later than 1780 or 1800, these vestibules may have been part of the original house design; but when found on any building earlier than these dates, there is usually reason to doubt that the vestibule is as old as the house.

Sometimes, in tearing down or altering an old house, the attachment of these vestibules to the house, and particularly in their under-floor and roof construction, becomes definite and plain. The basement wall usually runs right across the space under the vestibule floor, with its exterior underpinning plainly in view. The floor sill, also, is found to butt up against the

HOUSE AT GLOUCESTER,
CAPE ANN, MASSACHUSETTS

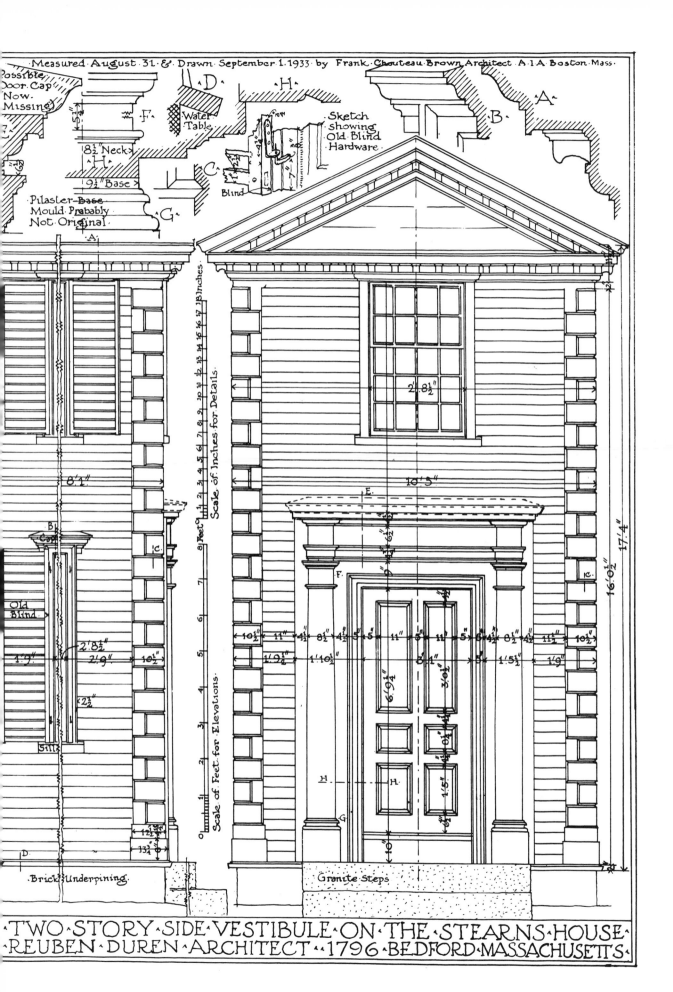

Measured August 31 & Drawn September 1.1933 by Frank Chouteau Brown Architect A.I.A Boston Mass.

Possible Door Cap Now Missing

·D·   ·H·

·F·   Water Table

Sketch showing Old Blind Hardware

·A·

·B·

8½ Neck

9½ Base

·C·

·G·

Blind

Pilaster-Base Mould Probably Not Original

·A·

Scale of Inches for Details.

2.8½"

8'1"

10'5"

E

Bl Cap

·C·

6½

F

Old Blind

1'9"

2.8½"

2'9"   10½"

10½" 11" 4½" 8½" 4½" 5 5 11" 5 11" 5 6 4½ 8½" 4½ 11½" 10½"

1'9½" 1'10½"   8'1" 5' 1'5½" 1'9"

6.9¼"   3.0½"

2½"

Scale of Feet for Elevations.

H   H

1'5"

Sill

G

6½

·D·

13¾"

1'0"

·Brick Underpining·

Granite Steps

TWO·STORY·SIDE·VESTIBULE·ON·THE·STEARNS·HOUSE·
REUBEN·DUREN·ARCHITECT··1796·BEDFORD·MASSACHUSETTS·

HOUSE ON BRIDGE STREET
SALEM, MASSACHUSETTS

many of the examples shown in this chapter, refer always to the period of the original house, rather than to the entrance vestibule itself.

These entrance vestibules also — as is equally true of other architectural details — usually develop marked local characteristics. In and about Salem, for instance, the vestibule ornamented at the corner angle by a rather heavy fluted Doric pilaster, without entasis, is the prevailing type. Possibly the side entrance to the well known Pierce-Johannot-Nichols House in Salem, attributed to McIntire, may have been the original, that was so often copied (some in very recent times!) by other builders, with a few easily managed modifications, all of classic conventionality of handling. In Gloucester a quite different type; wider, shallower; with side and arched toplights, seems to be the prevailing mode. In Marblehead a taller, narrower, more picturesque and informal sort of composition, indicates the less formal character of life and conditions then in vogue in that town. Andover has developed a vestibule type with square side windows set within an arch or impost motive of classical derivation. On Cape Cod a simple narrow flat pilaster, single or paired, is the prevailing style of vestibule door enframement; and every other district or town center

now exhibits its chosen local variation.

And so it goes. Outer projecting vestibules are found in a few earlier dwellings, such as the Col. Paul Wentworth Mansion at Salmon Falls, New Hampshire, built about 1701; or the old Cooper-Austin House in Cambridge, of some forty years earlier date (1657). And while these houses show vestibules of the simplest hipped-roof type; yet they are both of probably much later date than the structures to which they are now found attached.

The simplest types were of course most appropriate to these earlier Tudor pitched roof dwellings, — just as the later, more ornate designs, with pedimented and ornamented face, or balustraded roof treatment, are usually found attached to houses of 1810 to 1825, where it is quite probable that they may have been a part of the original plan and construction. And the same might be said of those more delicately molded and ornamented extensions, such as the two vestibules from Gloucester, one with the leaded glass side and top lights, that equally announce a similar date for their workmanship. In this case, the entire entrance was changed, probably to admit more light to the stairway hall, as well as to secure added space in the hall passage in front of the stairs.

HOUSE AT 121 BRIDGE STREET
SALEM, MASSACHUSETTS

HOUSE AT 52 ESSEX STREET, SALEM, MASSACHUSETTS

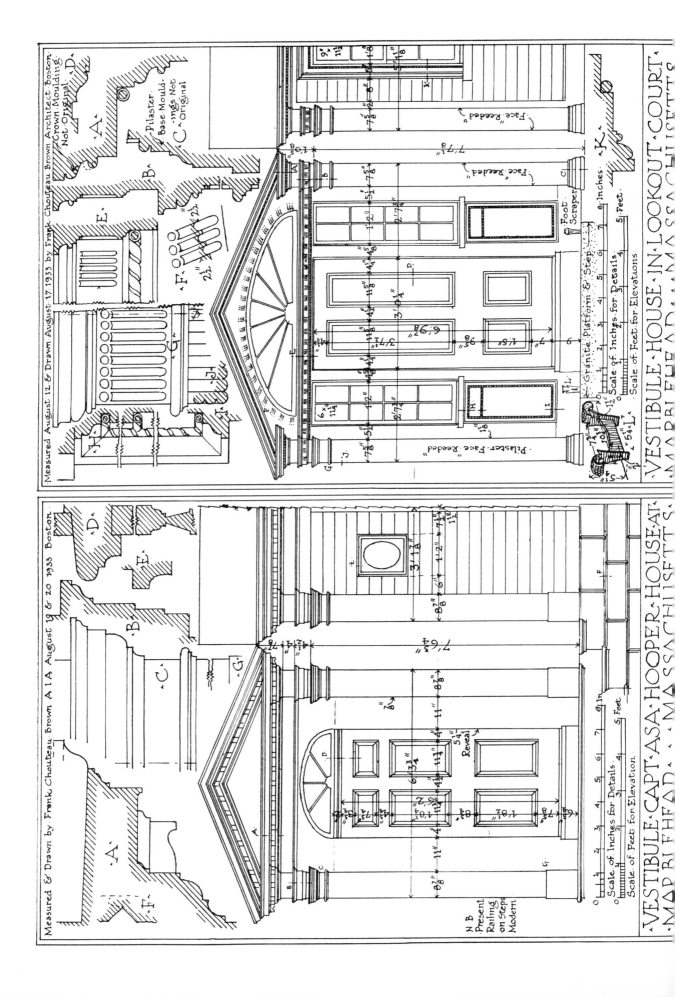

VESTIBULE · HOUSE · IN · LOOKOUT · COURT ·
MARBLEHEAD · MASSACHUSETTS ·

VESTIBULE · CAPT · ASA · HOOPER · HOUSE · AT ·
MARBLEHEAD · MASSACHUSETTS ·

HOUSE IN LOOKOUT COURT
MARBLEHEAD, MASSACHUSETTS

CAPT. ASA HOOPER HOUSE
MARBLEHEAD, MASSACHUSETTS

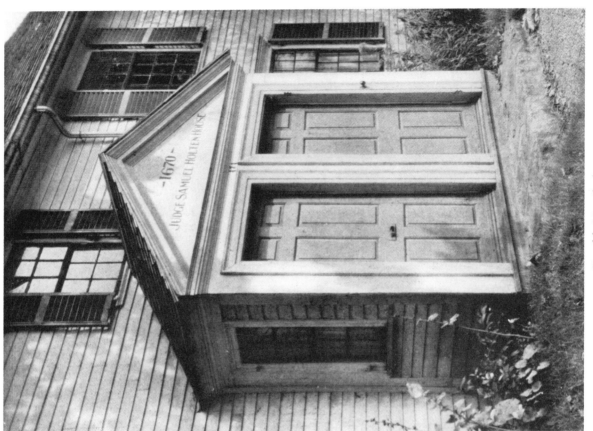

Double Vestibule
JUDGE HOLTEN HOUSE — 1670 —

Side Vestibule
HOUSE ON WASHINGTON SQUARE

·DOUBLE·VESTIBULE·JUDGE·HOLTEN·HOUSE·
·DANVERS·CENTER·1670·MASSACHUSETTS·

·SIDE·VESTIBULE·WASHINGTON·SQUARE·
·SALEM· ·MASSACHUSETTS·

Scale of Feet for Elevations·   Scale of Inches for Details·

Measured Sept 10 & Drawn Sept 15 1933 by Frank Chouteau Brown A I A

·Scale·of·Feet·for·Elevations·
·Scale·of·Inches·for·Details·

·Door·Handle· ·in·Brass·

Measured & Drawn September 10 & 12 1933 by Frank Chouteau Brown Architect·

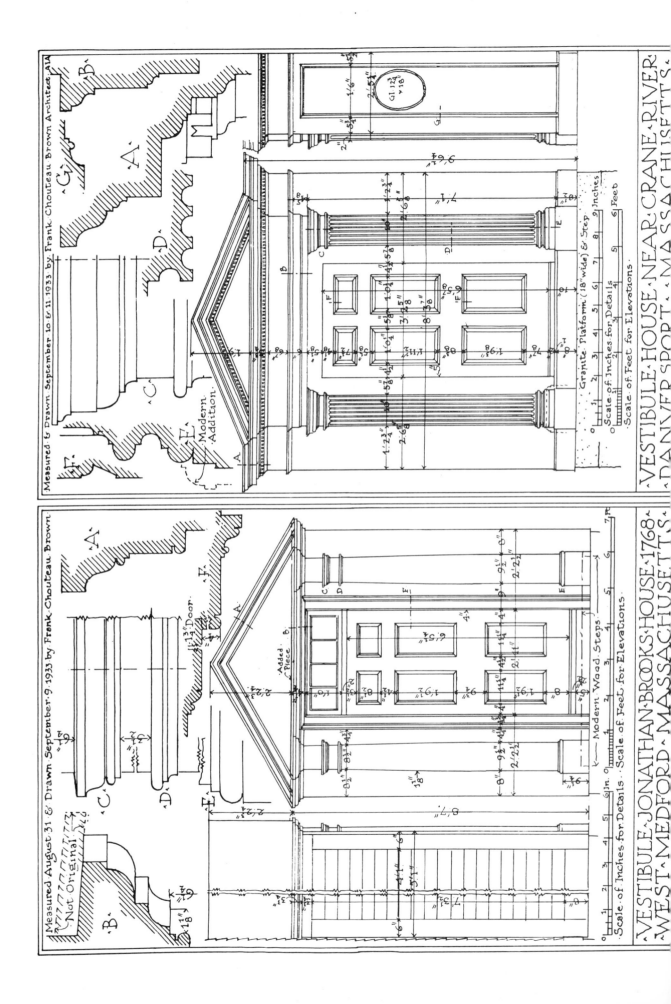

Measured & Drawn September 10 & 11 1933 by Frank Chouteau Brown Architect AIA

·Modern· Addition·

· Granite · Platform· (18" wide) & Step·

Scale · of · Inches · for · Details ·

· Scale · of · Feet · for · Elevations ·

·VESTIBULE·HOUSE·NEAR·CRANE·RIVER·
·DANVERSPORT·· ·MASSACHUSETTS·

Measured August 31 & Drawn September 9 1933 by Frank Chouteau Brown

·Not Original·

·Added· ·Piece·

·13" Door·

←—— Modern· Wood· Steps·

· Scale · of · Inches · for · Details · · Scale · of · Feet · for · Elevations ·

·VESTIBULE·JONATHAN·BROOKS·HOUSE·1768·
·WEST·MEDFORD·MASSACHUSETTS·

HOUSE NEAR CRANE RIVER
DANVERSPORT, MASSACHUSETTS

JONATHAN BROOKS HOUSE —1768—
WEST MEDFORD, MASSACHUSETTS

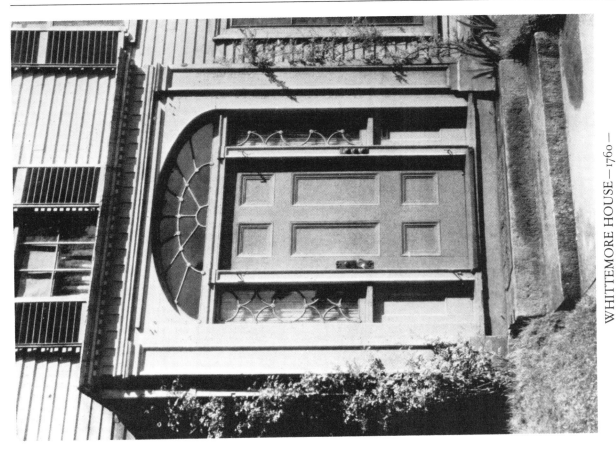

WHITTEMORE HOUSE — 1760 —
TOWN HALL SQUARE, GLOUCESTER, MASSACHUSETTS

HOUSE ON MIDDLE STREET
GLOUCESTER, CAPE ANN, MASSACHUSETTS

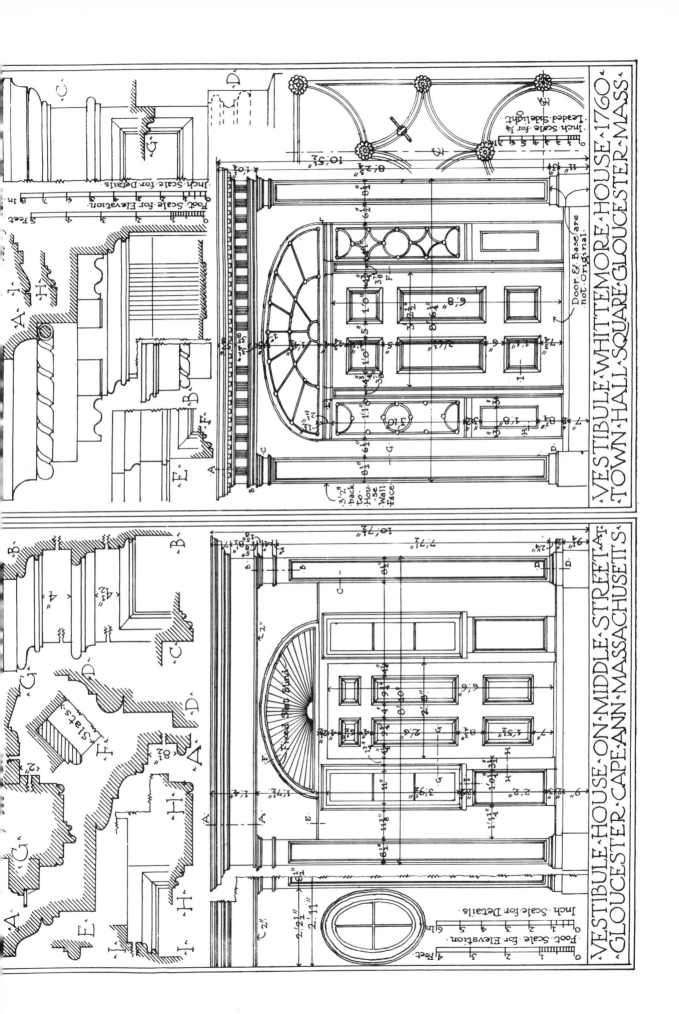

·VESTIBVLE·WHITTEMORE·HOVSE·1760·
·TOWN·HALL·SQVARE·GLOVCESTER·MASS·

·VESTIBVLE·HOVSE·ON·MIDDLE·STREET·AT·
·GLOVCESTER·CAPE·ANN·MASSACHVSETTS·

SAMUEL BROCKELBANK HOUSE — 1670 —
GEORGETOWN, MASSACHUSETTS

HOUSE AT 26 NORMAN STREET
SALEM, MASSACHUSETTS

HOUSE AT 23 SUMMER STREET
SALEM, MASSACHUSETTS

PEIRCE-NICHOLS HOUSE — 1782 —
SALEM, MASSACHUSETTS
Samuel McIntire, Architect

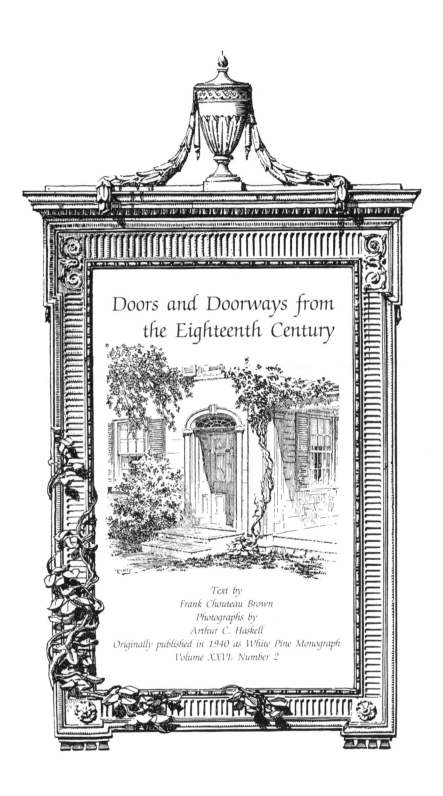

Doors and Doorways from the Eighteenth Century

Text by
Frank Chouteau Brown
Photographs by
Arthur C. Haskell
Originally published in 1940 as White Pine Monograph
Volume XXVI, Number 2

Doorways in Corner of Dining Room
FIRST HARRISON GRAY OTIS HOUSE — 1795 — BOSTON, MASSACHUSETTS
Charles Bulfinch, Architect

EXAMPLES OF INTERIOR DOORS AND DOORWAYS FROM THE EIGHTEENTH AND NINETEENTH CENTURIES

IN Early Interior Doorways in New England, Vol. X, Chap. 10, a number of earlier door types are illustrated, along with a number of six- and eight-paneled framed doors. In nearly every instance, however, the small panel there is found at the top of the door, which is—as a matter of fact—its most usual location, especially in the later years of the colonial period.

In this chapter, a few middle period doors have been selected to show other six-panel types, but now with the smaller panel in the middle of the door's height, along with a less usual instance of a door one panel wide and three in height. (And, to increase its individuality, the middle panel is divided into two in width!) Beyond this instance, several other examples of six-panel doors, now with the longest panel at the top, are illustrated. Most of these, again, will be found to date from the rather early and middle periods of New England's architectural development—although it must be remembered that we are always likely to find "sport" examples, evidencing some local custom, or the distinct effect of some dominating individual influence or school!

An unusual and marked example is the four-panel door from the Ruggles-Woodbridge House, in South Hadley, Massachusetts, where, in various rooms, the doors are differently treated or "jogged," both in the design of the panel outlines and also in the treatment of the architraves and backbands. It should also be noted that these panels and panel moulds are both "raised," or built against the face of the framed door styles.

Especially vital in the architectural effect of this important detail of the dwelling, is the method of "framing" or enclosing the door. In part, this may depend upon the structural method intended to hang the movable part of the design. The early batten door was hung with wrought iron strap hardware, placed against the face of the door, with iron nails driven through the cross batten upon the back, and "clinched" to make secure. The hinge was hung

over a pin driven into the adjoining panel strip, of which the door's face was a part, or secured in a nearby post of the house frame. The "strike" of the door frame into which the panel swung was made as simply as by adding a two-inch strip across the top of the opening and two sides, against which the swinging panel would rest when closed.

The early development of a framed door, in northern New England, apparently jumped the transitional type that is found in great variety in early houses along the lower Hudson Valley, and in parts of New Jersey and Pennsylvania. In New England, as elsewhere, the earliest doors were generally made of the same wide featheredged boards as usually formed the inside wall of the first wooden dwellings built in this region. Sometimes it was made from a single piece of pine, twenty-six to thirty-four inches wide; sometimes of two or three pieces battened together upon the outer, or back, side of the opening. In the latter case, in New England, the wider board is placed most frequently in the center, and narrower pieces, apparently cut from the wider sections forming the wall on either side of the opening, complete the necessary width. In the Hudson Valley region, it is more usual to find the center piece of the valve the narrowest, placed between two wider boards extending out to meet the sides of the door frame. In that region, too, this door is often set into a heavy interior masonry wall, instead of forming a part of a wooden partition along the inner room side. The cross battens—in New England usually two in number, and about four inches wide placed four to eight inches from the top and bottom of the door—are more frequently three in the Hudson Valley doors, where they are much wider and are often joined together with upright pieces strengthening the sides of the door, so that actually the effect of two panels is secured on what remains still, generally, the "back" of the door. The paneled effect is strengthened by the moulding that, more often than not, surrounds the inside of the space enclosed by

Original Glazed Door—"KING" HOOPER
HOUSE—1745—MARBLEHEAD, MASSACHUSETTS

these battens. In the prevalent Dutch door type, the wide center batten is split, so that half strengthens each part of the door.

In upper New England, at least, this "false paneled" effect is seldom found, although it appears to be a natural intermediate link between the plain batten and the framed and paneled door—so often of two panels only, in the earlier houses—almost all restricted to the early eighteenth century, or the few years immediately preceding it. In New England these early paneled examples are generally of genuinely framed and paneled workmanship, even though they are not over an inch in thickness.

Immediately following the batten "door," the opening was framed with two of the upright planks of the interior partition, which were finished on the sides toward the opening and rabbetted along that edge, while a "header" or cross piece, similarly treated, was fitted in between these uprights to finish across the top of the opening. A raised moulding, or backband, was then broken or mitred around the whole frame about two to three inches back from the door, against which the plaster or paneling of the wall finished. A little later—early in the nineteenth century—the upright studs forming the wall construction were used

only to enclose a rough opening, within which was set a heavier separate door frame, into which the door would fit. The latter was now heavier and thicker, and hung from hinges fastened into the rabbet, instead of on the face of the door frame. The space between the door and the rough construction of the partition was covered with a moulded façure board, of four to five inches width, and again backed with a heavier moulding,—which now covered the joint between plaster and wood, or made this separation between the materials more definite. It was first given a "bolection" type of surface outline,—and then shortly assumed its more customary later enframing section.

From this point onward the decorative advance was rapid. All sorts of fluted, carved, and moulded designs were employed upon the face of the applied finish treatment about the framed door opening. Pilasters were added at the sides, and frieze and cornices across the top to make an architectural cap or "overdoor"—to add grace, beauty and importance to the principal doorways within the better type of later Colonial dwelling.

Set within all this embellishment the door itself also

Door—GAY MANSE—c1795—
SUFFIELD, CONNECTICUT

was gradually becoming more varied in material and treatment. Sometimes walnut or mahogany were substituted for the simpler painted pine of earlier work. Sometimes both were combined, one for the stiles, the other for the panels. Sometimes the moulding separating the two was of still another material, such as ebony. And along with this the early years of the nineteenth century saw more panels added in height and width, in a greater variety of design and proportion. More elaborate panel moulds, of finer section, came into use and were often elaborately worked. The edge of the raised part of the panel developed its own moulded treatment. It was stopped, and then curved, — or broken at the corner angles. Or another edging mould was set in upon the face of the enclosed panel, and the space between was sometimes grooved or otherwise decoratively and appropriately treated.

At some time very soon after 1800 the moulding, that had formerly been run along the inner edges of the door stiles, was made separately, and the panel was fitted into a groove in the stile edge, the moulding being added afterwards to hold the panel in place.

Then the double door was tried on the interior, to

Door—RUGGLES-WOODBRIDGE HOUSE—1788—
SOUTH HADLEY, MASSACHUSETTS

join — or to separate — two adjoining parlors, or a parlor from a wide hallway. At first it was hinged to swing, but it was soon arranged to slide back out-of-sight into the partition, — or to fold back into and become one of the sides of a paneled vestibule or alcove. For all of this, new and special types of hardware were employed, which would require another and separate article — all by itself.

Another unusual door is the partly-glazed door from the "King" Hooper House at Marblehead; and an example from the Peter Jayne House in the same town, displays a portion of the old stenciled border. In Marblehead and Danvers, stencils were used more in the form of borders, rather than in the all-over pattern shown in the Frost Farmhouse — just over the Maine border, at Eliot — that was popular in that region.

Turning to later and more decorative examples, the door and window from the Jerathmael Bowers House, in Somerset, shows a treatment derived partly, at least, from nearby Rhode Island influence, and of about thirty years later date than the dwelling itself. A stiff and heavy "overdoor" treatment appears in the Gen. Salem Towne House (for the window design, see Vol. X, Chap. 9); while the door and doorhead from the Stevens-Tyler House in Andover, attributed

Door—CAPT. SAMUEL TREVETT HOUSE—C1750—
MARBLEHEAD, MASSACHUSETTS

Door — PETER JAYNE HOUSE — c1724 — MARBLEHEAD, MASSACHUSETTS

Door — MAJOR CHARLES FROST HOUSE — c1730 — EAST ELIOT, MAINE

Hall Door — COOK-OLIVER HOUSE — 1804 — SALEM, MASS.
Samuel McIntire, Architect

Doorway in Dining Room — JARATHMAEL BOWERS
HOUSE — 1770 — SOMERSET, MASSACHUSETTS

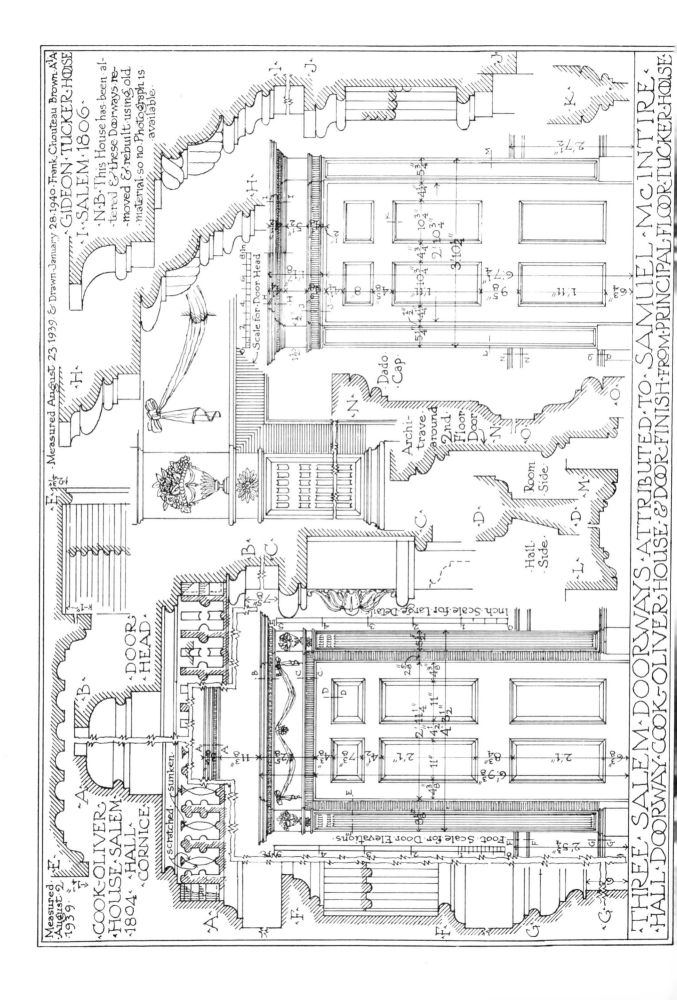

THREE·SALEM·DOORWAYS·ATTRIBUTED·TO·SAMUEL·McINTIRE·
HALL·DOORWAY·COOK·OLIVER·HOUSE·&·DOOR·FINISH·FROM·PRINCIPAL·FLOOR·TUCKER·HOUSE·

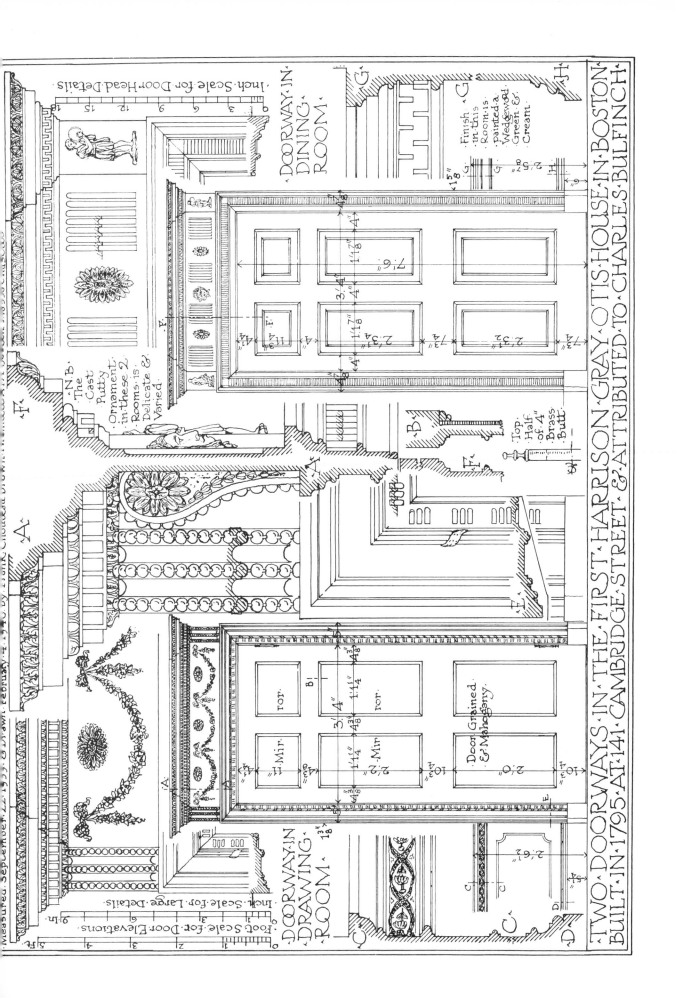

· TWO · DOORWAYS · IN · THE · FIRST · HARRISON · GRAY · OTIS · HOUSE · IN · BOSTON ·
BUILT · IN · 1795 · AT · 141 · CAMBRIDGE · STREET · & · ATTRIBUTED · TO · CHARLES · BULFINCH ·

· DOORWAY · IN · DINING · ROOM ·

Finish in this Room is painted a Wedgewood Green & Cream.

· N.B. · The Cast Putty Ornament in these 2 Rooms is Delicate & Varied.

Top Half of 4" Brass Butt.

· DOORWAY · IN · DRAWING · ROOM ·

Door Grained & Mahogany.

Mir. ror. / Mir. ror.

Inch Scale for Door Head Details

Inch Scale for Large Details

Foot Scale for Door Elevations

Samuel McIntire, Architect   *Door Head in East Parlor*
PEIRCE-NICHOLS HOUSE — 1782 — SALEM, MASSACHUSETTS

Charles Bulfinch, Architect   *Door Head in Drawing Room*
FIRST HARRISON GRAY OTIS HOUSE — 1795 — BOSTON, MASSACHUSETTS

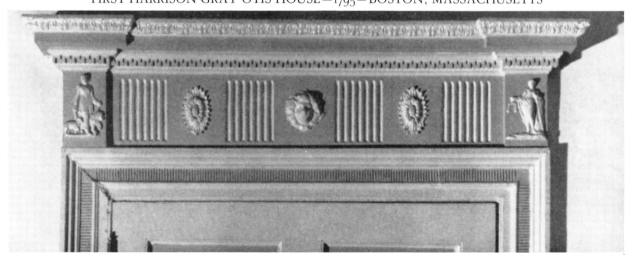

Charles Bulfinch, Architect   *Door Head in Dining Room*
FIRST HARRISON GRAY OTIS HOUSE — 1795 — BOSTON, MASSACHUSETTS

Doorways in Corner of Drawing Room
FIRST HARRISON GRAY OTIS HOUSE — 1795 — BOSTON, MASSACHUSETTS

to McIntire, is less graceful than his Salem work.

The Cook-Oliver House was built by Captain Samuel Cook in 1804, but some of its interior finish and the gateposts are believed to have been taken from the Elias Haskett Derby House, when it was demolished to make room for the Town House, several years later. A similar factor influenced the Peirce-Nichols House, which, although built in 1782, was not completed until 1801, when the eastern half shows a far more delicate

width—are all from that locality. (Another is illustrated in Volume IX, Chapter 15.)

Elaborate doorway treatments are found in the first Harrison Gray Otis House, by Charles Bulfinch, now headquarters of the Society for the Preservation of New England Antiquities. The variety of the cast putty ornaments—where the same detail is rarely repeated—appears with similar ornament in other mantels and details, near Boston. Other over-

(Courtesy of Essex Institute Collection)

Double Doorway—CAPT. EBENEZER SHILLABER HOUSE—c1800—SALEM, MASS.
Samuel McIntire, Architect

McIntire treatment, including the carved doorheads.

Double-width doors, for interior locations, are not usual in Colonial work, but Salem provides us with a number of examples. Remembering its early Theatre, as well as its many early ballrooms, connecting parlors, or wide hall openings met a social need, while means of closing them in winter were equally important. The several examples—one of unusual

door treatments are the McIntire door caps from "The Larches," in Cambridge (in Vol. VII, Chap. 9); crocketed door caps (Vol. VI, Chap. 14) from the John Brown House, 1786, Providence; or the Carrington and Warren House (Vol. VI, Chap. 5)—while to understand the full relation of the Custom House door cap detail to the balance of the design, the reader is referred to Vol. X, Chap. 8.

Door Head in Entrance Hall
CUSTOM HOUSE — 1819 — SALEM, MASS.

Door Head in Ballroom
TOWN HOUSE — 1816 — SALEM, MASS.

Door Head in Dining Room
HARRISON GRAY OTIS HOUSE — 1795 — BOSTON

(Courtesy of Historic American Buildings Survey)
Door Head in Entrance Hall
COOK-OLIVER HOUSE — 1804 — SALEM, MASS.

Double Doorway at End of Ballroom
OLD TOWN HOUSE — 1816 — SALEM, MASSACHUSETTS

Double Doorway — FORMERLY IN JOSEPH PEABODY
HOUSE — 1820 — SALEM, MASSACHUSETTS

Doorway – STEVENS-TYLER HOUSE – c1800 –
NORTH ANDOVER, MASSACHUSETTS

Door – GEN. SALEM TOWNE HOUSE – 1796 –
CHARLTON, MASSACHUSETTS

Doorway in Main Hall
COLEMAN-HOLLISTER HOUSE — 1796 — GREENFIELD, MASSACHUSETTS
Asher Benjamin, Architect

Interior Arched Openings found in Northeastern Colonial Work

Text by
Frank Chouteau Brown
Photographs by
Arthur C. Haskell
Originally published in 1940 as White Pine Monograph
Volume XXVI, Number 5

Doorway with Oval Toplight in Entrance Hall
EDWARD CARRINGTON HOUSE — c1811 — PROVIDENCE, RHODE ISLAND

SOME INTERIOR ARCHED OPENINGS FOUND IN NORTHEASTERN COLONIAL WORK

THE use of the arch form as interior decorative detail executed in wood, while not exactly frequent in New England, nevertheless seems to have been employed quite often—particularly in those houses having the most architectural importance. To be of any magnitude, it is perforce limited to houses of an unusually high stud, especially when used to span wider distances, or when employed in anything approaching a semi-circular form. Its most frequent early uses were, perhaps, in terminating the upper part of the corner cupboard (to which more particular attention will be directed in the last chapter), but it was also sometimes used for interior round-topped doorways—as in the Warner House at Portsmouth—1722 (Vol. X, Chap. 10). Sometimes these archways were filled with glazed doors or sash, as in the double doorway from the Lee-Nichols House in Cambridge; or the upper part of the wall cupboard from the Elisha Smith House, in Stillwater, Rhode Island. For more pretentious toplight examples, the elaborately glazed arched opening in the George Read, II, House, from New Castle, Delaware, or the doorway in the Music Room of the John Brown House at Providence (Vol. VI, Chap. 14), with the semi-circular tympanum filled with an elaborately carved pattern in wood relief, might serve as illustrations.

The circular or elliptical cross-hall archway—especially in the Southeastern coastal regions—has always been a favorite employment, either to suggest a separation of a rear from a front continuous hallway; to set apart a recess containing a stairway from the main open hall—though with less frequency of use—for an opening between a hall and a main first floor room, or even to partly join or connect a front and a rear parlor.

In demarking a staircase recess, it has even been used in a doubled form, as in Gunston Hall, Fairfax County, Virginia (Vol VIII, Chap. 6) and in the entrance hallway of "Tulip Hill," Anne Arundel County, Maryland (Vol. II, Chap. 2). In yet another southern mansion, Wye House, in Talbot County, Maryland (Vol. VIII, Chap. 2), flattened and elliptical arched top openings were used in several instances—along the hallway, as well as between adjoining rooms.

In the George Read, II, House at New Castle, Delaware (Vol. IV, Chap. 9) not only was the hallway interrupted along its length by two large and elaborately decorated semi-circular archways; but a number of richly patterned glass toplights were used to fill arched openings extending over the wide doorways between interior rooms, as well as above the entrance. These interior doors with arched toplights might be considered even as an endeavor to both "have one's cake and eat it too"; to secure the richness of the arch feature, while at the same time maintaining separation of the rooms. An even more naive use is seen in the Jonathan Woodbridge House (page 187), built in a still more northern clime—in Hampshire County, Massachusetts—in 1806. Here the necessity for conserving heat during a large part of the year probably motivated the arrangement—which was obviously planned and built all at the same time; to separate a front from a rear hall, where the staircase was located off the rear hall space, and therefore the need for a practicable connection existed the year around.

In fact, it must by now have become apparent that the location of the archway in the hall is perhaps its most universal usage. A number of examples from northeastern locations are illustrated in the chapter given to staircases and entrance hallways (Vol. X, Chap. 11). In this location—midway the hall's length—the archway is usually elliptical, and actually serves to focus interest upon the stairway, located behind it, that it thus visually enframes and emphasizes.

Among the considerable number of cross-hallway arches shown in that chapter are those in the Sarah Orne Jewett, Col. Isaac Royall, Jerathmael Bowers, and Capt. Gregory Purcell houses, along with the quite unique example/ from the Coleman-Hollister House. While the John Vassall House, in Cambridge, supplies still another example (Vol. VII, Chap. 9) that, most unusually, springs from brackets on the side walls of the hall that, in their turn, are set against the faces of small paneled pilasters extending from the floor.

Even more frequently, the arched top opening is found utilized in New England in a location under the upper run of the main stairway —or under its intermediate wide landing—thus providing both a special feature in the lower hallway and a partial support for the stairway construction thrown across above it. Instances of its use in this location have also been illustrated rather frequently within recent years, and another example, from the Saltonstall House; demolished some twenty years ago, at Haverhill, Mass., is here shown as it appeared, both from the front hall as well as looking through the archway from the further entrance.

Besides this limited yet distinctive group, usually found in dwellings dating from the middle of the eighteenth century; with the beginning of the century following, there appear a few smaller types that possess unusual charm and delicacy of detail and treatment. Instead of springing across a wide central hallway, at a location in front of the end hall staircase — these smaller archways are placed at the opening of side or intersecting corridors, that allowed them to be both narrower and smaller in scale than the more sturdy and wider-flung ones that had preceded them. While the former type actually often

Arched Toplight to Closet
39–40 BEACON STREET — 1818 —
BOSTON, MASSACHUSETTS

Arched Recess Formerly in Rear Parlor
AMORY-TICKNOR HOUSE — 1804 — BOSTON, MASS.

performed a structural purpose, in concealing a heavy cross beam or tie, these later types are used almost exclusively for their decorative value; and the four examples— pages 183–186—of different dimensions, proportions and detail, all attributed to Samuel McIntire, are those that have been used as models for most of the variants derived from them.

The use of arches upon each side of a central fireplace, to cover recessed alcoves, is also found in a few New England dwellings. Sometimes it is as simple and bold a treatment as in the 1780 portion of the Col. William R. Lee House at Marblehead (Vol. III, Chap. 9) where it is most unusually a full half-circle in outline; or, more usually, as an elliptical arch, in the example from an old Charlestown, Massachusetts, house (page 192) that was in process of demolition even as these measurements were being taken, in 1934. In this instance, the same general treatment was employed in two separate parlors—in the one the archways framed recessed windows, and in the other, doorways. A still more ornate and elaborate treatment was employed in the West Parlor of the Vassall-Craigie - Longfellow House, 1759, at Cambridge, Mass. (Vol. VII, Chap. 9), as well as in the Sargeant - Murray - Gilman - Hough House, 1768, at Gloucester, Mass. (Vol. III, Chap. 13), while the builders of the Royall House, at Medford, utilized similar—

though simpler—motives on more than one of its floors.

In the Gloucester house just mentioned, as was also the case in another old house—now in use as the Gloucester Town Library—a single circular headed window was placed directly in the center of the hallway over the main stair landing. This employment was similar to that in the Sarah Orne Jewett House, at South Berwick, Maine (Vols. X, Chap. 9, and IX, Chap. 11), while, in a still more elaborate and decorative form the series already illustrates what are probably the best two examples in New England—in the Jeremiah Lee Mansion, at Marblehead (Vol. X, Chap. 12), and in "The Lindens," formerly at Danvers (Vol. X, Chap. 9).

And still other uses for circular sash openings have been devised. To light an inner closet, a semi-circular toplight, a circular window (or even an octagonal one!) can be employed. While, in plan, the slightly recessed niche with arched top, commonly used for a statuary figure, occurs in many hallways of the early nineteenth century.

Archway to Parlor Alcove
92 WASHINGTON SQUARE, SALEM, MASS.

Archway to Parlor Extension as Remodeled about 1799
HUNTINGTON HOUSE—1752—HADLEY, MASSACHUSETTS

Arched Double Doorway
LEE-NICHOLS HOUSE — 1660 — CAMBRIDGE, MASSACHUSETTS

Arched Wall Cupboard
ELISHA SMITH HOUSE, STILLWATER, RHODE ISLAND

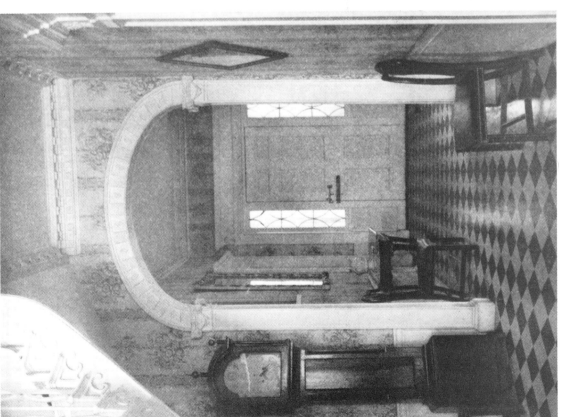

Archway, Staircase Hall to Second Floor Rear Corridor

Archway, Staircase Hall to First Floor Rear Entry

GARDNER-WHITE-PINGREE HOUSE — 1804 — SALEM, MASSACHUSETTS

Samuel McIntire, Architect

Courtesy Pennsylvania Museum of Art, Philadelphia

Further Arch Relocated in McIntire Room, Philadelphia Museum

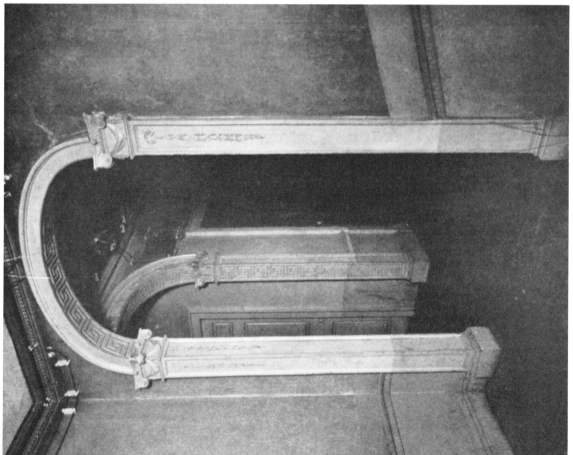

Courtesy Essex Institute

Hall Archways in Original Location, before Removal

ARCHES—FORMERLY IN EZEKIEL HERSEY DERBY HOUSE—1799—SALEM, MASSACHUSETTS

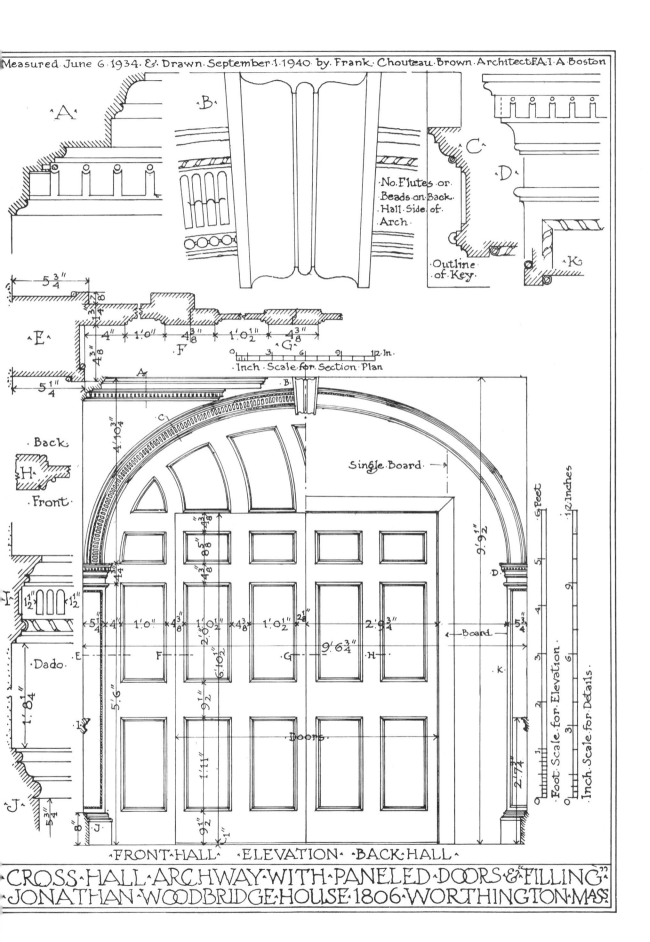

Measured June 6 1934 & Drawn September 1 1940 by Frank Chouteau Brown Architect F.A.I.A. Boston

·A·

·B·

·C·

No. Flutes or
Beads on Back
·Hall·Side·of·
Arch

·D·

Outline
·of·Key·

·K·

5 3/4"

·E·

4" 1'·0" 4 3/8" 1'·0 1/2" 4 3/8"

·F· ·G·

0   3   6   9   12·In.

·Inch·Scale·for·Section·Plan·

5 1/4"

·Back·

·H·

·Front·

A

B

C

Single Board

9'·9 1/2"

·Dado·

4'·10 3/4"

8 5/8"

1'·8 1/4"

D

E   F   G   9'·6 3/4"   H

Board

k

5 6"

2'·0 1/2"

6'·10 1/2"

1'·0 1/2"   2 1/8"   2'·9 3/4"

5 1/4" 4" 1'·0" 4 3/8"

·Doors·

2'·7 1/4"

1'·4 1/4"

9 1/2"

·J·

5 3/4"   8"   J   9 1/2"   1"

6 Feet

Foot Scale for Elevation.

12 Inches

Inch Scale for Details.

·FRONT·HALL· ·ELEVATION· ·BACK·HALL·

CROSS·HALL·ARCHWAY·WITH·PANELED·DOORS·&·"FILLING"
JONATHAN·WOODBRIDGE·HOUSE·1806·WORTHINGTON·MASS

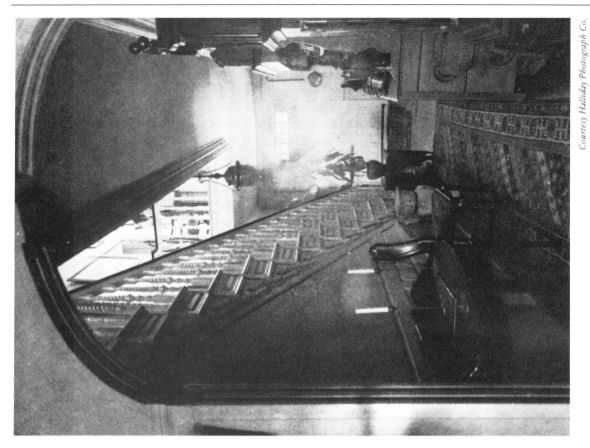

Courtesy Halliday Photograph Co.

Staircase Hall, seen through Archway from North Entry

Staircase Hall and Archway to North Garden Entrance

HALL UNDER STAIR ARCHWAY – SALTONSTALL HOUSE – 1788 –

Double Doorway with Semi-Circular Toplight
GEORGE READ, II, HOUSE — 1799 — NEW CASTLE, DELAWARE

Doorway with Elliptical Arched Toplight
HOUSE AT 92 WASHINGTON SQUARE, SALEM, MASS.

Dining Room End Toward Fireplace with Arched Side Alcoves

Dining Room End Showing Central Sideboard Alcove
JERATHMAEL BOWERS HOUSE — 1770 — SOMERSET, MASSACHUSETTS

Dining Room End with Paneled Arched Recesses
ROCK HALL — 1767 — LAWRENCE, LONG ISLAND, NEW YORK

Drawing Room End with Arched Recesses to Front Parlor
"ELMWOOD" — 1760 — CAMBRIDGE, MASSACHUSETTS

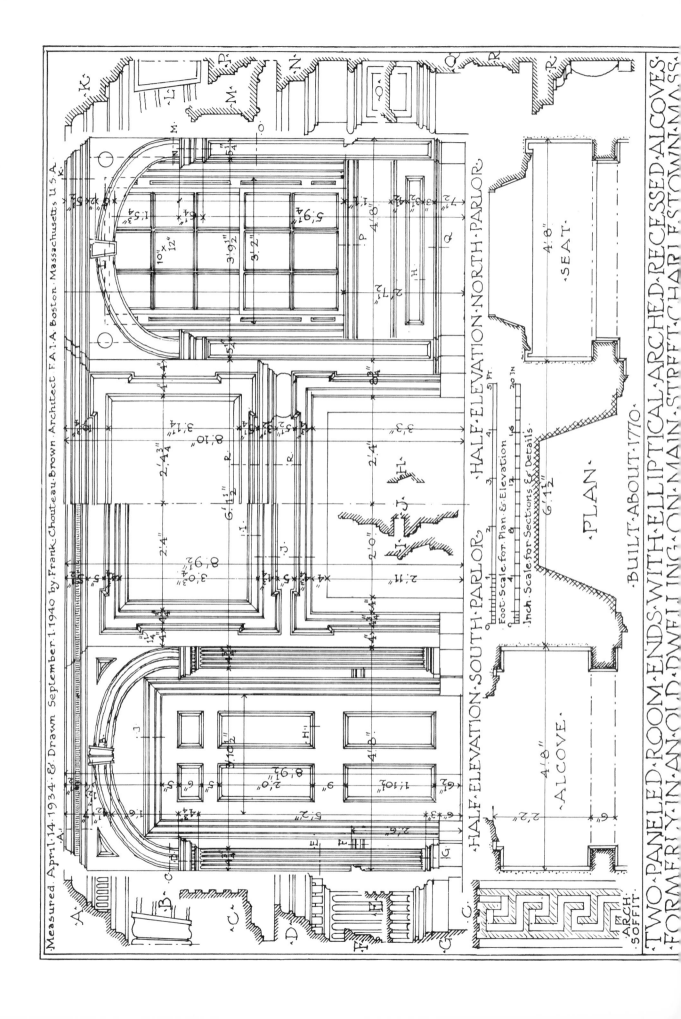

TWO·PANELED·ROOM·ENDS·WITH·ELLIPTICAL·ARCHED·RECESSED·ALCOVES·
FORMERLY·IN·AN·OLD·DWELLING·ON·MAIN·STREET·CHARLESTOWN·MASS·

Low Mantels and Fireplace
Enframements from
the Nineteenth Century

Text by
Frank Chouteau Brown
Photographs by Arthur C. Haskell
Originally published in 1939 as White Pine Monograph
Volume XXV, Number 5

Mantelpiece in Front Parlor
MAJ. ISRAEL FORSTER HOUSE — 1804 — MANCHESTER, MASSACHUSETTS

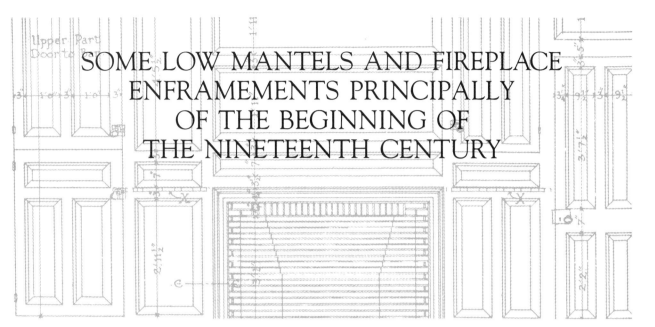

SOME LOW MANTELS AND FIREPLACE ENFRAMEMENTS PRINCIPALLY OF THE BEGINNING OF THE NINETEENTH CENTURY

AT the time the fireplace was removed from its earlier location in the center of the room to one of its walls or corner angles, the square hearth shrank to a segment of its former area; and its marginal moulding seems, appropriately enough, to have extended upward over the wall surface in order to continue to limit the fireplace boundaries along its two sides and top. In those medieval days when the fire recess was first given an enclosed or concealed flue, it usually opened from the top of a stonebuilt hood, which itself soon became an appropriate part of the aesthetic design of the mantel, as well as exercising its inner functional purpose in collecting the smoke above the firebox and directing it into the flue that had been newly devised for the very practical purpose of removing the smoke from the room.

As the firebox itself became more deeply recessed into the wall—and especially as that wall became less a part of a stone built border castle and came into general use in the more humble dwelling of serf or retainer—the somewhat pretentious exterior hooded treatment disappeared from view; although it remained concealed more deeply within the wall, and was executed in humbler—and less fire resisting materials. In this less costly and more impermanent dwelling, the fireplace was either only partially built of stone inserted into a wooden or wattle wall,—or it largely or entirely filled one end of the principal room of the small dwelling; the flue often being carried up outside, of crisscrossed twigs heavily daubed with wet clay both inside and out.

This was also the earliest method employed in New England, and survivals of this treatment may still be found in early houses along the Eastern Coast, of which perhaps the best known examples are the early "stone-end" houses of New Jersey, Connecticut, and

Rhode Island—or the brown stone dwellings of the lower Hudson Valley. When the house increased in size upon the ground, however, it became a matter of economy in construction, as well as in the conservation of heat and fuel, to place the chimney in the center of the small structure, thus enclosing the chimney and increasing the danger of fire, as well as bringing it between the inner walls of the two or three room floor plan. The chimney at once became larger, the fireplaces deeper, and the masonry construction of the fireplace itself came necessarily to be extended up through the wooden framed structure and well above its roof surfaces.

At the same time the fireplace began gradually to shrink in size, both in width—or length—height and depth. As this tendency continued, the aesthetic requirements of the owners (or perhaps it was only the woman's demand for simpler surfaces to clean and dust) introduced a wooden screen or partition that filled the remainder of these interior walls, separated the staircase and hall from the two or more rooms on each floor—and made necessary some sort of a boundary or lapping finish that would cover the point where the masonry fireplace stopped and the wood boarded wall at each side of and over it began. And so—and from quite another and different set of conditions— once again the suggestion for a moulded enframement of the fire opening evolved.

The danger of fire was still sufficient to require that the masonry firebox be extended in a façure upon both sides, and over the top of the fire opening, in the wall face; that the bordering woodwork be kept well back from the fire opening, and that a moulding be introduced to make tight the joint between the two materials and prevent any draft from drawing sparks up back of the paneling, into the space around and outside of the chimney flue. Among the earliest treatments, was the well known form of the bolection moulding, at first used along the edge of the fire opening in stone, and later reproduced in wood (but at first still maintaining a full stone scale) four to eight inches back from the edge of the fire opening.

In some early fireplaces this precaution was disregarded, and an example may be seen in the West Paneled Bedroom of the Col. Paul Wentworth Mansion (Vol. IX, Chap. 13). This was a rather dangerous exception, nevertheless—as not only might sparks from the fire be carried in back of the paneling, but also the inner edge of the wood stiles come so near the edge of the masonry opening that the heat from a hot fire might easily start a conflagration.

In most cases, therefore, the early fireplaces in Colonial dwellings were placed back of a paneled end or side wall of a room, with a framing moulding around the fire opening. In other words, the rudiments of what is termed a "mantel." The earlier simple bolection moulding, which often fitted back against the stile of a paneled wall treatment, was often

PINE·DRAWING·ROOM·OLD·MANTEL·
COL·PAUL·WENTWORTH·ELEAZER·ARNOLD·
MANSION·SALMON·FALLS·HOUSE·LINCOLN·
NEW HAMPSHIRE· RHODE·ISLAND·
TWO·EARLY·LOW·MANTELPIECES·

Old Mantel
DR. PETER OLIVER HOUSE — 1762
MIDDLEBOROUGH, MASSACHUSETTS

aided by some especial emphasis on the area directly over the fireplace opening (Vol. IX, Chap 13) usually by a simple variation in the direction or arrangement of the panelwork itself. The bolection section was supplanted by other simple moulded arrangements—as is illustrated in Vol. IX, Chap. 13), and at the left, where the mouldings of that example are drawn.

A simple variant of the label moulding is often used without a shelf over it (although the latter is frequently added in later years—as in Vol. IX, Chap. 13), returning against a plain paneled wall in the earlier years, or—a little later—against a wall of plaster—as in the Dr. Peter Oliver House (below) and the Stephen Daniel House (opposite). By early in the eighteenth century the use of plaster surfacing for at least three of the room walls became common, although the fireplace wall still continued to be paneled. The first change was to retain the high mantel with overpanel to the ceiling, sometimes with flanking side pilasters; but extending the plaster over the balance of the fourth wall, as well. This form was most typical of the English Georgian period, and was fashion-

Old Mantel in Later "End Leanto" Portion — c1740 —
ELEAZER ARNOLD HOUSE — 1687 — LINCOLN, RHODE ISLAND

(Historic American Buildings Survey)

Mantel in First Floor South West Room (Older Portion)
STEPHEN DANIEL HOUSE — 1693 — SALEM, MASSACHUSETTS

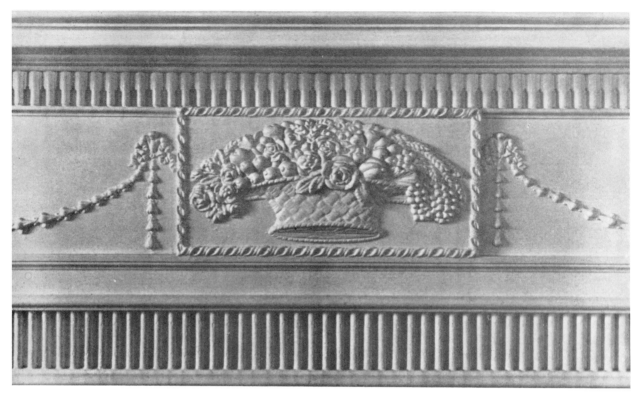

Details of Frieze and Pilaster Ornament, Parlor Mantel
MAJ. ISRAEL FORSTER HOUSE—1804—MANCHESTER, MASSACHUSETTS

ably followed in this country. But there being no longer a structural reason for the high mantel, it began by the end of the century to disappear. The new fashion was to continue the lower portion of the preceding form, with well established mantel shelf, and leave the wall space above it open for the hanging of a fine portrait or mirror.

An early example of this simple type is in the end-addition made to the Eleazer Arnold House (page 197),—a dwelling which is also one of the best examples of the Rhode Island "stone-end" fireplace house plan (Vol. VI, Chap. 13). Another simple—and rather early—example is in the Col. John Gorham House (page 200). This is the type that has continued a favorite down to the present day. Embellished, as it has been, by small pilasters, by carved panels and frieze decorations, by carpenter's hand worked and chiseled grooves, by varied and flowing cutlines, it is the type to which the other illustrations in this issue have been given.

Two early examples of the new pilaster supports are in the Bryant-Cushing House, page 202 (Vol. X, Chap. 13). An example of a transitional type from the preceding "over-mantel panel," on page 194, is shown; where two delicate pilasters extend from the lower mantel shelf to the cornice of the room. The influence

Details of Carving, McIntire Mantel, The "Lindens," formerly at Danvers, Massachusetts
TAKEN FROM THE NATHAN READ HOUSE—1790—DEMOLISHED IN SALEM, 1856

of Samuel McIntire is clearly evident in this mantel,—and, as Maj. Forster came from Marblehead to settle in Manchester, there may be reason for this resemblance—although its charming delicacy contrasts strongly with the bedroom mantel drawn beside it on page 202! Incidentally, the wall paper on this parlor was ordered by the owner from England, and, along with papers on the Dr. Oliver, and Samuel Fowler rooms, show five early examples in this issue. Another McIntire mantel is the sole survivor of the Salem over-door and three mantels from the Nathan Read House (Salem, 1790) that were installed in the "Lindens" by Francis Peabody on his purchase of the place in 1860 —even against its incongruous 1754 paneled breasts!

In the Samuel Fowler mantels, pages 204 and 205, reappear the same local hand-cut and turned "carpenter patterns," to which notice was directed in the details of the doorways shown in Vol. VII, Chap. 3. Equal ingenuity is displayed by Cape Cod workmen at the Christopher Ryder House at Chathamport, who, with their grooved chisels, worked otherwise plain surfaces into partially fluted and beaded treatments.

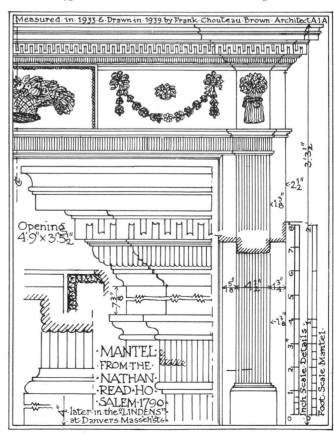

(Historic American Buildings Survey)

McIntire Mantel, from Nathan Read House — 1790 — Salem

LATER IN "THE LINDENS," AT DANVERS, MASSACHUSETTS

Dining Room Mantel

COL. JOHN GORHAM HOUSE — 1690 — BARNSTABLE, MASS.

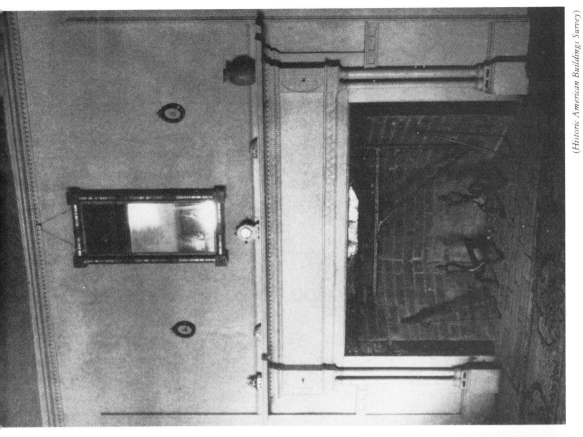
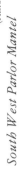

(Historic American Buildings Survey)

South West Parlor Mantel

(Historic American Buildings Survey)

Mantel in Bedroom

CHRISTOPHER RYDER HOUSE—1809—CHATHAMPORT, MASSACHUSETTS

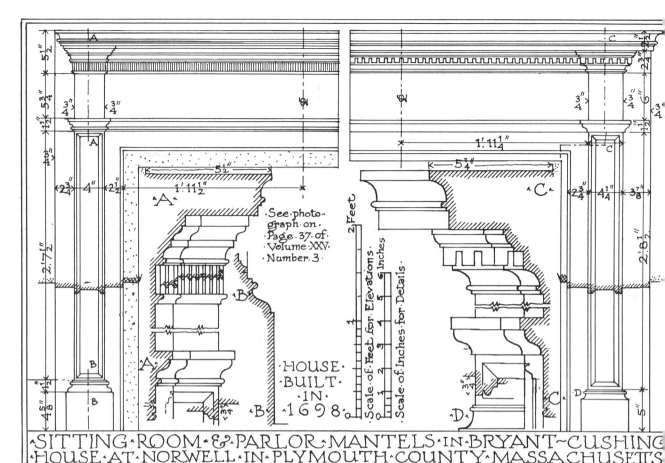

See photo-
graph on
Page 37 of
Volume XXV
Number 3

HOUSE
BUILT
IN
1698

Scale of Feet for Elevations
Scale of Inches for Details

SITTING·ROOM·&·PARLOR·MANTELS·IN·BRYANT~CUSHING·
HOUSE·AT·NORWELL·IN·PLYMOUTH·COUNTY·MASSACHUSETTS

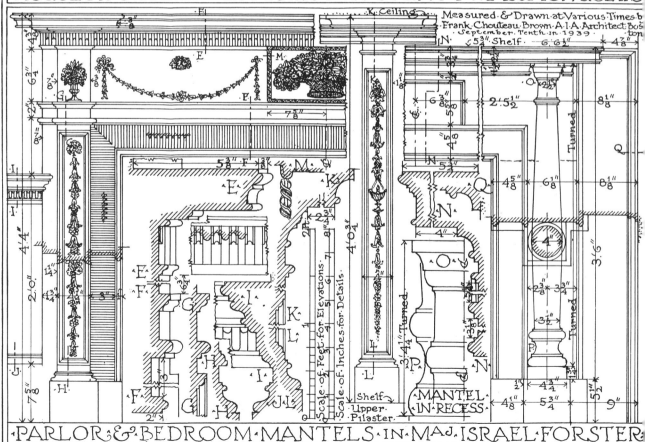

Measured & Drawn at Various Times by
Frank Chouteau Brown A.I.A. Architect Boston
September Tenth in 1939

Shelf

K Ceiling

MANTEL
IN RECESS

Scale of Feet for Elevations
Scale of Inches for Details

Shelf
Upper
Pilaster

PARLOR·&·BEDROOM·MANTELS·IN·MAJ·ISRAEL·FORSTER·
HOUSE·1804·AT·MANCHESTER·IN·ESSEX·COUNTY·MASSACHUSETTS

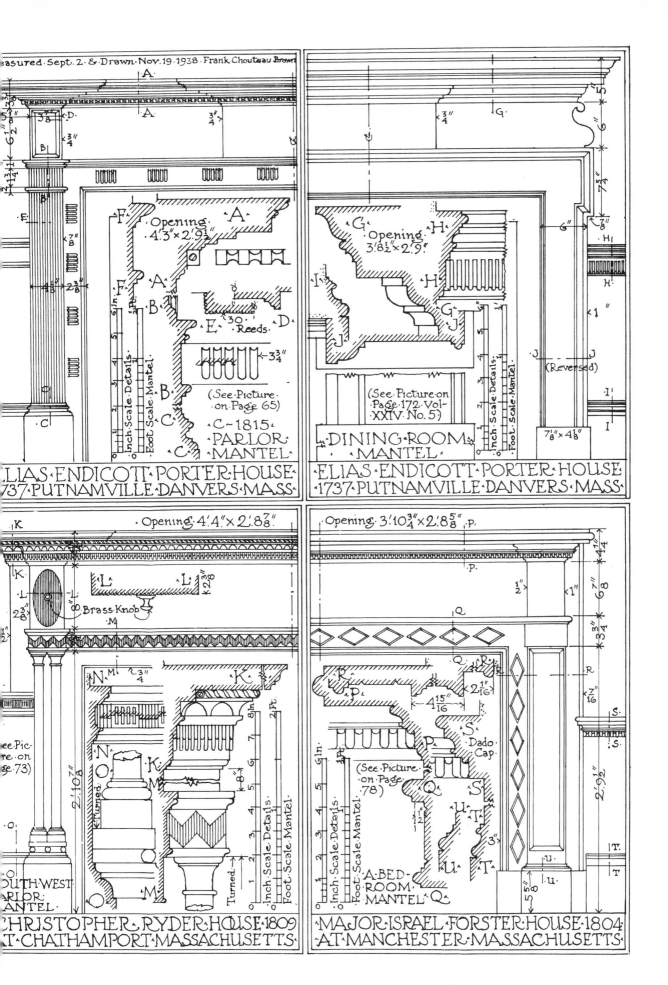

Measured·Sept·2·&·Drawn·Nov·19·1938·Frank·Chouteau·Brown

Opening·4'3"×2'9¾"
A
F
A
B
E ·30· Reeds·
D
B
C
(See·Picture· on·Page·65)
C~1815·
PARLOR· MANTEL
·Inch·Scale·Details·
·Foot·Scale·Mantel·

ELIAS·ENDICOTT·PORTER·HOUSE· ·1737·PUTNAMVILLE·DANVERS·MASS·

Opening· 3'8½"×2'9"
G   H
I   H
J   G
J   J (Reversed)
(See·Picture·on Page·172·Vol· XXIV·No.5)
DINING·ROOM· MANTEL
7⅛"×4⅛"
·Inch·Scale·Details·
·Foot·Scale·Mantel·

ELIAS·ENDICOTT·PORTER·HOUSE· ·1737·PUTNAMVILLE·DANVERS·MASS·

Opening·4'4"×2'8⅞"
K
K
L   L
Brass·Knob
M
N   M
N   K
O
M
2'10⅞"
Turned
ee·Pic- re·on ge·73)
OUTH·WEST· ARLOR· ANTEL
·Inch·Scale·Details·
·Foot·Scale·Mantel·
Turned

CHRISTOPHER·RYDER·HOUSE·1809 ·T·CHATHAMPORT·MASSACHUSETTS·

Opening·3'10¾"×2'8⅝"·P·
P
Q
Q   R
R   R
P
Dado Cap·
S
(See·Picture· on·Page ·78)
P   Q
S
U   T
A·BED· ROOM· MANTEL·Q
4¹⁵⁄₁₆"   2¹⁄₁₆"
5⅝"
2'·9½"
·Inch·Scale·Details·
·Foot·Scale·Mantel·

MAJOR·ISRAEL·FORSTER·HOUSE·1804· ·AT·MANCHESTER·MASSACHUSETTS·

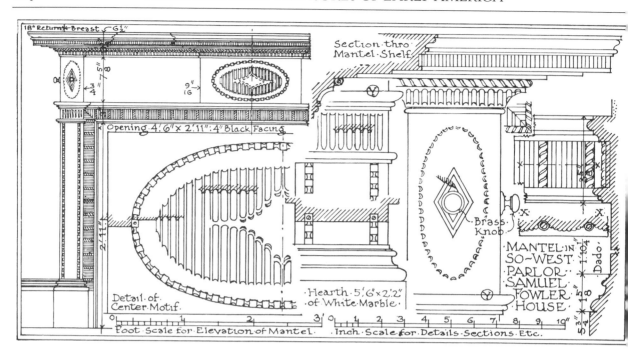

Mantel in South-West Parlor
SAMUEL FOWLER HOUSE — 1810 — DANVERS, MASSACHUSETTS

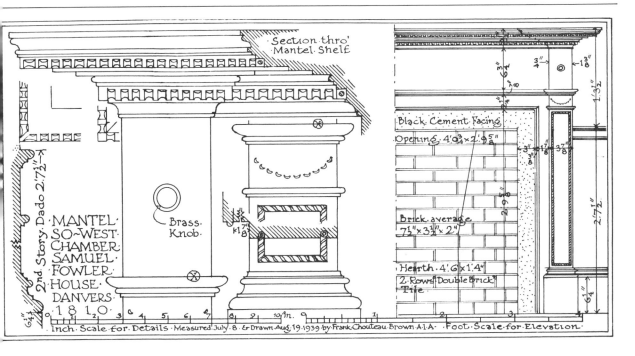

Mantel in South-West Chamber
SAMUEL FOWLER HOUSE — 1810 — DANVERS, MASSACHUSETTS

Mantel in Bedroom

Mantel in Bedroom
MAJ. ISRAEL FORSTER HOUSE — 1804 — MANCHESTER, MASSACHUSETTS

Mantel in Bedroom
EDWARD EVERETT HOUSE — 1806 — CHARLESTOWN, MASSACHUSETTS

Bulfinch Type Mantel in Parlor
MAYOR ADAMS HOUSE — 1811 — CHARLESTOWN, MASSACHUSETTS

Kitchen Fireplace and Mantel
OLD TAVERN INN — c1700 — SOUTH MIDDLEBOROUGH, MASSACHUSETTS

Kitchen Fireplace and Mantel
ELIAS ENDICOTT PORTER FARMHOUSE — 1737 — PUTNAMVILLE
DANVERS, MASSACHUSETTS

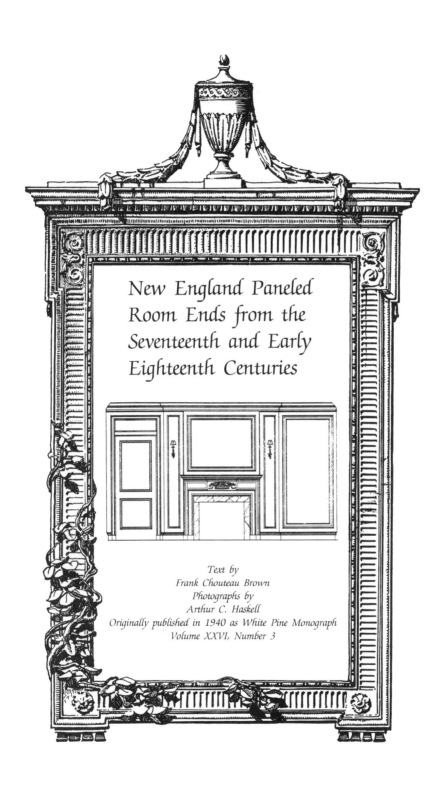

New England Paneled Room Ends from the Seventeenth and Early Eighteenth Centuries

Text by
Frank Chouteau Brown
Photographs by
Arthur C. Haskell
Originally published in 1940 as White Pine Monograph
Volume XXVI, Number 3

Paneled End in Southwest Room, First Floor
WADSWORTH HOUSE — 1726 — CAMBRIDGE, MASSACHUSETTS

SOME NEW ENGLAND PANELED ROOM ENDS FROM THE SEVENTEENTH AND EARLY EIGHTEENTH CENTURIES

THE general prevalence of the paneled wall along one side of the room interior, where the fireplace is located, is widely established in most residential structures of the seventeenth and eighteenth centuries in New England. Its origin derives from the principal typeplan of the one-room with fireplace at one end, or the two-room floor plan with central chimney, that is almost universally found employed in early dwellings in that region. In either case, three sides of the room were along the exterior wall of the building.

A house built before 1660 by one of the wealthiest men in the Plymouth Colony, when taken down and removed to a new location about twelve years ago, revealed that the original oak frame was covered with one and one-eighth inch, wide oak boards, extending from the sill to the plate for the full two stories of the dwelling's height, with wide "shadow mouldings" along both edges of the inside face of the boards. They were indubitably intended to be exposed as the finish wall of the rooms inside.

This same sort of construction was used in Connecticut, in a building of as late date as 1820, where, however, the space between the rough natural edges of the boarding was plugged with lime mortar, and then split lathing nailed against the inner face of the wall and finish-coated with plaster.

On the other hand, both in that state and in Massachusetts, as well as others in New England, we have the early custom of placing the original split oak clapboards directly upon the exterior uprights of the old oak frames (without the use of any exterior boarding), the wall facing of the room inside being then either plastered on split laths, often six to eight feet long, nailed to the inner face of the frame; or sometimes faced on the interior with wide horizontal pine boarding, with featheredge or lapped joints. An instance of a dwelling, built in 1649, illustrates the former method. In that particular case, the space between the studs was filled with puddled clay, probably from the inside as the split lath boards were added course over course. The clay was fluid enough

to work out and fill up the spaces between the lapping oak rived clapboards, which were probably also plugged up with moist clay from the exterior, to insulate the wall and keep it tight against weather and cold.

On the face of the fourth, or inner wall of the room, the problem that confronted the early builders was entirely different. Here they were only concerned with surfacing the wall so that the unsightly bulk and rough clay daubing of the chimney stack would be concealed, but at the same time so that all the heat from flues and fireplaces would be left to radiate through the interior of the dwelling on all its floors and attic, for its full height. And as the need for fuller insulation against the cold New England winters became more and more important with each succeeding generation, the better insulation of plaster came to be accepted for use inside all the exterior walls of the dwelling (especially as limerock sources were discovered and worked more generally in the different settlements), while the transmittal of heat through the open pores of the wooden walls upon each side of the chimney stack and its clustering fireplaces was also generally appreciated. This was especially true before the painting of interior woodwork became fashionable. This period seems to vary in different sections, the earlier dates being about 1750, while many interiors are known to have been left in the natural wood, without paint, up to as late as a hundred years later. As the earlier paints used resembled rather thin pigment stains, they did little to fill the pores of the woods or prevent the passage of heat. But with the general use of heavier pigments, such as lead, as a protecting surface, of course the wood pores were entirely closed.

It should also be remembered that much of the paneling now found in early houses was not installed at the date given for the original construction of the dwelling, but in most cases was added many years later. The use of wide pine boards with feather or grooved edges for covering room walls was general in New England during the seventeenth century.

Paneled Wall in Southeast Room, First Floor   H.A.B.S.

COL. RUGGLES WOODBRIDGE HOUSE — 1788 — HADLEY, MASS.

Paneled End in West Bedroom   H.A.B.S.

GEORGE WARD HOUSE — 1712 — LAKEVILLE, MASSACHUSETTS

Near the end of that period—or early in the years that followed, raised panels, placed against the face of framed stiles, and held in position by some sort of bolection-shaped moulding, are frequently found, and in some sections this style is seen in dwellings built even after 1750. But meanwhile, the use of tall narrow panels, with a wide rail to stiffen the wall just below the middle of its height, began to supplant earlier methods, or even, in many cases, was applied upon the face of earlier paneling. This became the most prevalent and generally used style, extending up nearly to the end of that century. Following this usage, the four walls of the rooms were more and more generally all plastered, and the Georgian type of mantel, with shelf and overmantel extending up to the room cornice, became the fashion, until the overmantel itself came to be discontinued shortly after the beginning of the nineteenth century.

The illustrations show a few examples of the earliest type of interior boarded wall surfacing (pages 214 and 220) that still remain unsullied by the addition of later paint coatings. Following this, came walls with applied or raised panels (page 215). This required a heavy moulding, that continued into later years as an emphasis to the overmantel panel (pages 209, 218, 219 and 224). Then came another form of covering border moulding (pages 212, 223, and 224); and, finally, the simpler panel moulding most commonly and widely used, which appears in all the panels on page 210, and in many other New England wall treatments. It is also characteristic that all the effect of this type of paneling is obtained without the use of any separate strip of moulding. The quarter-round itself is run along the inner

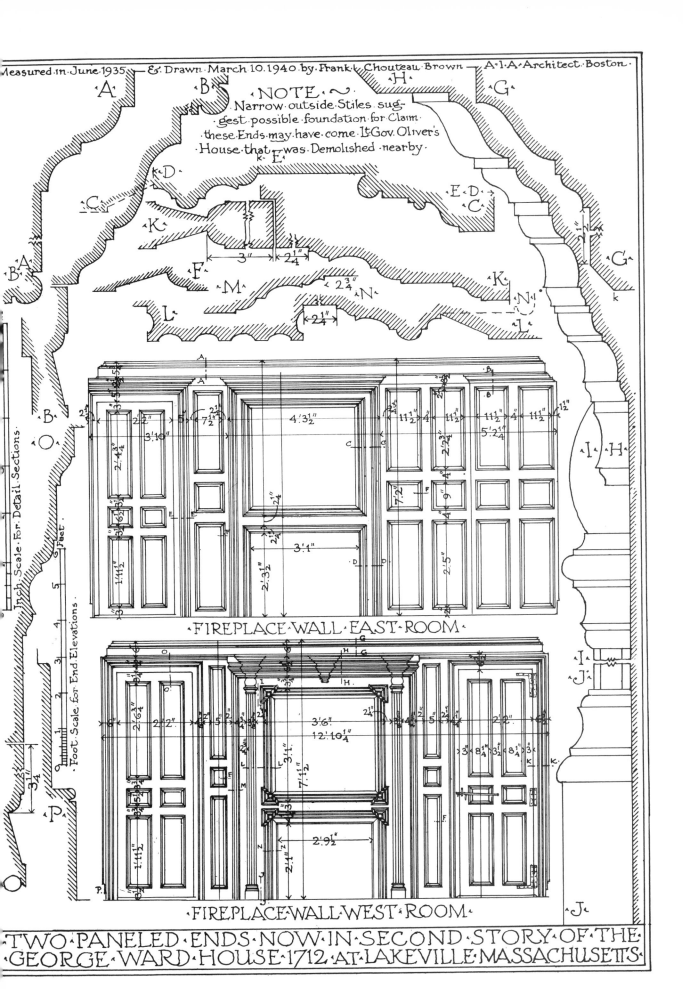

Measured in June 1935 · & · Drawn · March 10. 1940 · by · Frank · Chouteau · Brown · A·I·A· Architect · Boston ·

· NOTE · ~
Narrow · outside · Stiles · sug-
gest · possible · foundation · for · Claim ·
these · Ends · may · have · come · Lt·Gov· Oliver's
House · that · was · Demolished · nearby ·

· FIREPLACE · WALL · EAST · ROOM ·

· FIREPLACE · WALL · WEST · ROOM ·

· TWO · PANELED · ENDS · NOW · IN · SECOND · STORY · OF · THE ·
· GEORGE · WARD · HOUSE · 1712 · AT · LAKEVILLE · MASSACHUSETTS ·

edge of the framed enclosing stiles, and the thin sloping border running around all four sides of the enclosed panel, intended to fit into the grooved edge of the stile, itself functionally completes the raised moulding panel section.

With one exception, 1760 is about the latest date of the houses whose interior wall treatments have been illustrated, and in later dwellings, of course, the paneling is far more likely to have been installed as part of the original finish. It is in the earlier dwellings that later interior paneled walls and mantels, and casing over of early structural beams and posts, are usually found.

(Historic American Buildings Survey)

Early Woodwork, South End of Kitchen Bedroom
BRYANT-CUSHING HOUSE — 1698 — NORWELL, MASS.

(Historic American Buildings Survey)

Paneled Fireplace Wall in Old Living Room
CUSHING HOUSE — 1720 — HINGHAM, MASSACHUSETTS

Paneled End, West Side of East Bedroom   (*Historic American Buildings Survey*)

SIMON BRADSTREET HOUSE—1667—NORTH ANDOVER, MASSACHUSETTS

Paneled End, West Side of East Bedroom   (*Historic American Buildings Survey*)

BENJAMIN ABBOT FARMHOUSE—1685—ANDOVER, MASSACHUSETTS

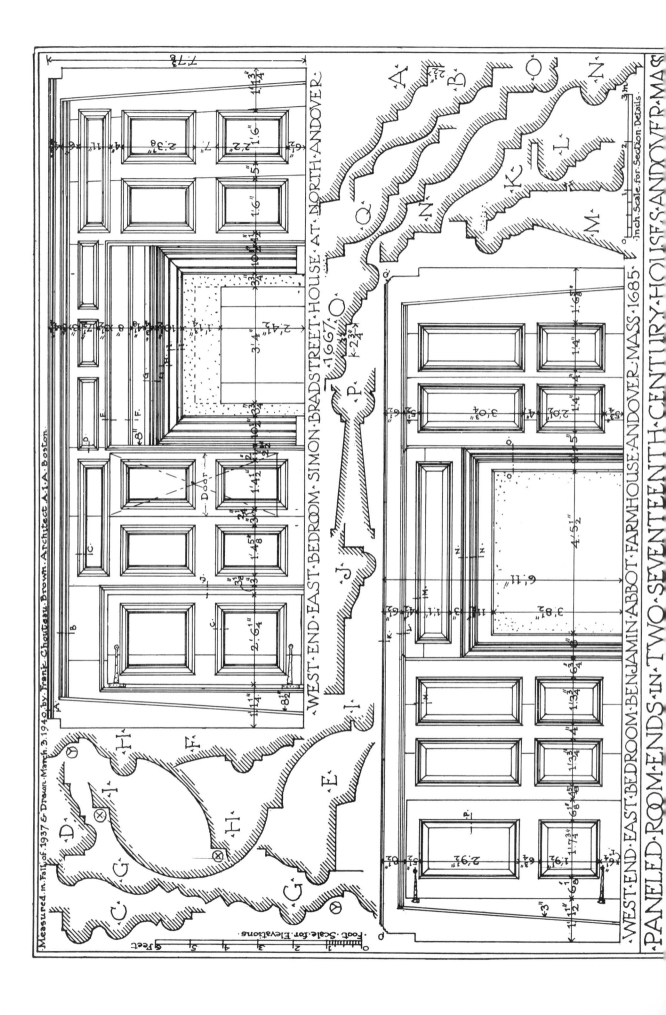

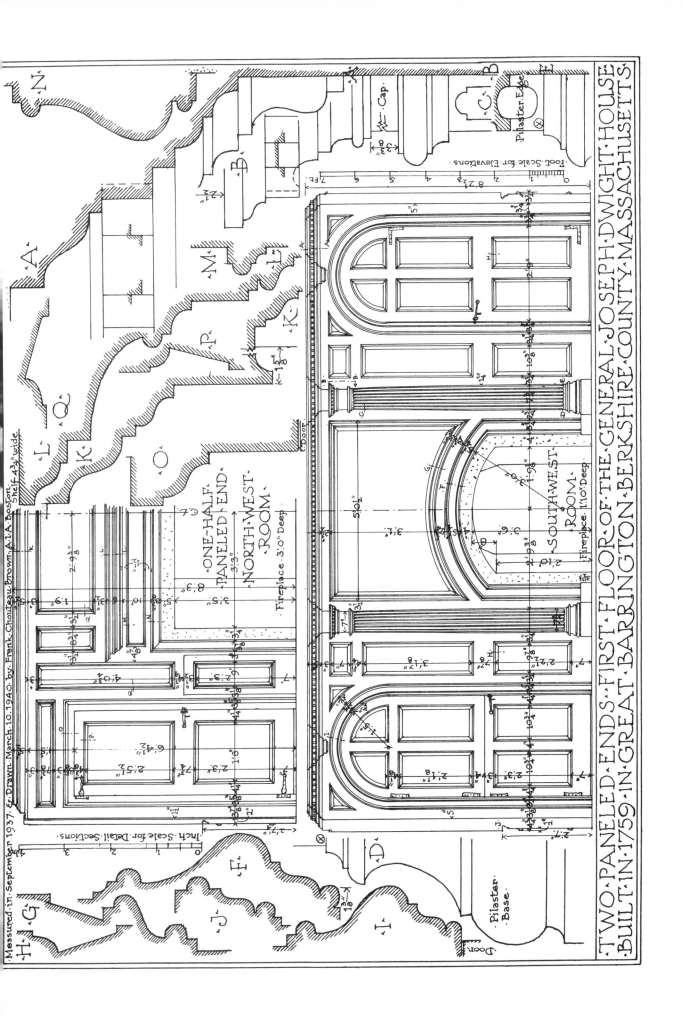

·ONE·HALF·
·PANELED·END·
·NORTH·WEST·
·ROOM·

Fireplace· 3'·0"·Deep·

·SOUTH·WEST·
·ROOM·

Fireplace· 1'·10"·Deep·

·Cap.·

·Pilaster·Edge·

Foot·Scale·for·Elevations·

·Measured·in·September·1937·&·Drawn·March·10·1940·by· Frank·Chouteau·Brown·A·I·A·Boston·

Shelf· 4¾"· wide·

Inch·Scale·for·Detail·Sections·

·Door·

·Pilaster·
·Base·

·Door·

·TWO·PANELED·ENDS·FIRST·FLOOR·OF·THE·GENERAL·JOSEPH·DWIGHT·HOUSE·
·BUILT·IN·1759·IN·GREAT·BARRINGTON·BERKSHIRE·COUNTY·MASSACHUSETTS·

Paneled End in Northwest Bedroom
CURTIS TAVERN — 1765 — GRANVILLE, MASSACHUSETTS

Paneled End in Southwest Parlor
GEN. JOSEPH L. DWIGHT HOUSE — 1759 — GREAT BARRINGTON, MASSACHUSETTS

Paneled End in Southwest Bedroom
COL. WILLIAM R. LEE HOUSE—1745—MARBLEHEAD, MASSACHUSETTS

Paneled End in Northwest Bedroom
JEREMIAH LEE MANSION—1768—MARBLEHEAD, MASSACHUSETTS

Portion of Paneled End in Old Hall

EMERY HOUSE — 1675 — WEST NEWBURY, MASSACHUSETTS

Detail of Paneled End in Living Room

SHORT HOUSE — c1732 — OLD NEWBURY, MASSACHUSETTS

Portion of Paneled End in Southwest Room, First Floor
JUDGE JOSEPH LEE-NICHOLS HOUSE—c1660—
CAMBRIDGE, MASSACHUSETTS

Detail of Paneled Wall in Southeast Room, First Floor
JUDGE JOSEPH LEE-NICHOLS HOUSE—c1660—
CAMBRIDGE, MASSACHUSETTS

(Historic American Buildings Survey)

Pine Paneled Wall in Southwest Room, First Floor

CAPTAIN SAMUEL TREVETT HOUSE — c1750 — MARBLEHEAD, MASSACHUSETTS

(Historic American Buildings Survey)

Grained and Paneled End in Southwest Room, First Floor

SQUIRE WILLIAM SEVER HOUSE — 1760 — KINGSTON, MASSACHUSETTS

Paneled End in Second Floor Room

(Historic American Buildings Survey)

OLD MARSHALL HOUSE — c1760 — BOSTON, MASSACHUSETTS

Paneled End in Northeast Room, Second Floor

(Historic American Buildings Survey)

JOSHUA ("WASHINGTON") WARD HOUSE — c1760 — SALEM, MASSACHUSETTS

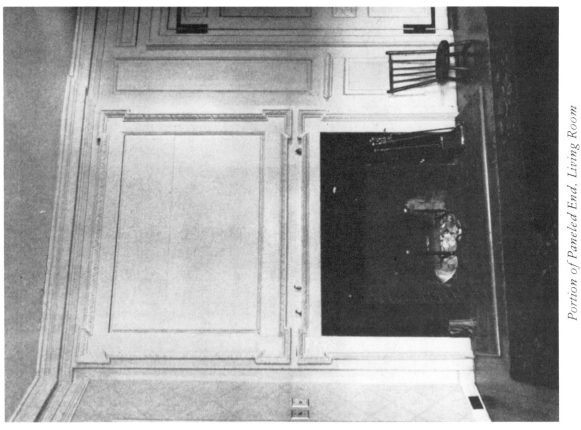

Portion of Paneled End, Living Room

COL. COOKE HOUSE – BEFORE 1730 – TIVERTON, R. I.

Detail of Paneled End in Bedroom

REV. EAST APTHORP HOUSE – 1760 – CAMBRIDGE, MASS.

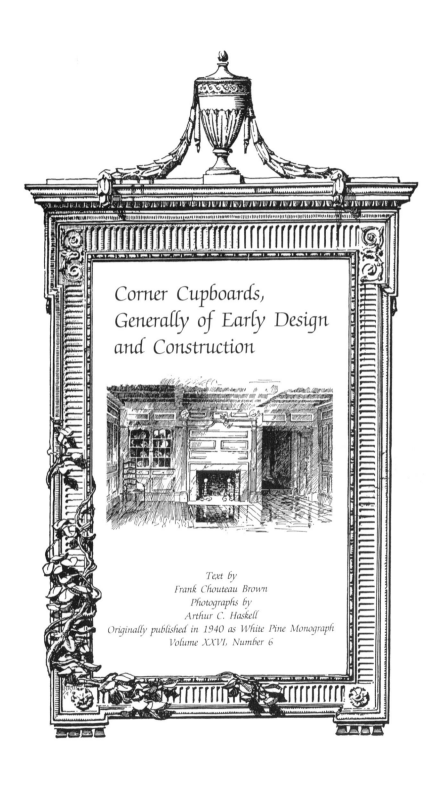

Corner Cupboards,
Generally of Early Design
and Construction

Text by
Frank Chouteau Brown
Photographs by
Arthur C. Haskell
Originally published in 1940 as White Pine Monograph
Volume XXVI, Number 6

Early Pine Circular-Top Open Corner Cupboard
HARTWELL FARMHOUSE, LINCOLN, MASSACHUSETTS

SOME EXAMPLES OF CORNER CUPBOARDS GENERALLY OF EARLY DESIGN AND CONSTRUCTION

A FTER the kitchen dresser, or wall cupboard so useful and necessary an adjunct to the early habitation in the Colonies that it seems almost to have been an initial fitment of every early dwelling, — the corner cupboard seems to have been next in demand by early housewives. And as the former was always located against the wall nearest the kitchen fireplace, the latter was usually so placed as to fill up an internal angle in the least used corner of the dining room. The former was an actual necessity to keep at hand the cooking utensils needed in the kitchen, and the latter was almost equally necessary to at once protect and display the few family heirlooms of pewter or china, of which the housewife was most proud. The early Colonial corner cupboard was, indeed, the direct family ancestor of the ugly Victorian corner whatnot of more recent memory!

Farther south it seems often to have been known as the *"Beau fait,"* or buffet; but along the northern coast it usually took a less pretentious name and form; — and, while retaining the fine proportions and outlines of its southern counterpart, it was generally made of more modest materials, and was better adapted to taking its place as an almost integral part of the walls of the dining room. Where the finish was natural pine, so also we find the corner cupboard beautifully fitted into this atmospheric background; or, if the walls of the room were painted and paneled — or even plastered — we continue to find that one or another varied treatment of the well-known arched-top motive is appropriate, and even unobtrusively decorative — in a quiet New England way! — in some unused but conveniently visible corner of the daily family habitat.

Corner Cupboard
SUDBURY, MASS.

Usually, in its simpler forms, the upper part of the cabinet was left open, with an arched, elliptical or segmental outline at the top; and the lower portion — up to about the height of the window sills or the room dado — had its shelves protected by paneled doors. Usually, the cupboard extended to the full height of the room, — fitting up against the ceiling, or into the beams or room cornice, in much the same way as did the early fireplace with overmantel treatment. But there were also simple corner treatments, with glazed or paneled doors shutting off the upper shelves from view, although by far the more customary and favorite design was to have the upper shelves protected by a glazed door or doors, with arched or segmental top, thus permitting objects placed upon the upper shelves easily to be seen at all times.

These glazed doors and arched tops were often enframed by a surrounding panel mould; or by side pilasters, tied into an entablature at the top; or fitting into the regular room cornice, whose mouldings would break out around or over the projecting pilasters or architraves flanking the opening. These pilasters were rather rarely of the full Georgian classic proportions, — but, in New England, were usually simpler and more attenuated, with but three or four flutings instead of the regulation seven, and often ended at top and bottom in other than the conventional cap and base of Classic precedent.

In plan, the problem of fitting shelving for the display of small objects was met by giving the cupboard a semi-circular back, and fitting the shelf outlines in the upper or more open part of the cupboard, to this circular plan, with the addition of a central projection at that point where the shelving was deepest.

Sometimes—in the more elaborate examples—this circular top arch was filled with a semi-domed treatment,—sometimes carried out in plaster, but more often in wood,—when the under part of this semi-dome was sometimes carved more or less skillfully into a conventional shell. The example shown from the Wiggin-Miller House (pages 226, 227, 233 and 234) is unusual in that, despite its successful expression of the shell-motive, it has been executed in the simplest possible way, by moulding rather than actual carving the built-up wooden back of the cupboard.

This typical semi-circular plan and design of the corner cupboard, once fully developed, was found adaptable to locations other than the inner corner of a room. It could be used recessed within a flat paneled wall, sometimes covered with a "blind paneled door," that was itself almost a unit of the wall paneling. Some very elaborate examples have been designed to meet this sort of a location,—as might be illustrated by referring to the wall cupboard in the well known "House of Seven Gables" at Salem (Vol. VII, Chap. 2).

Detail, Carved Shell Top of Cupboard
WIGGIN-MILLER HOUSE, STRATHAM, N. H.

The two cupboards shown on page 232 represent a type where perhaps some local carpenter was attempting to suggest the appearance of the shell-topped cupboard, by introducing this scalloped effect around the inner edge of the semi-circular outlined top of the upper recess. This is more probably the case with the left-hand example. That upon the right of the page developing a sophistication and skill of design, that quite transcend any suggestion of shallow imitation.

The two straight-top types on page 230 are of less usual design. In the case of that shown at the right, it is probable that the low ceiling of the room forced both the width and omission of even the elliptical arched top,—and, while this is not the case with the other example, here, too, the unusual width of the design,—as well as the use of paneled doors to enclose the upper shelving, indicates definite reticence and individuality on the part of its builders.

Most of the examples shown here are early types, some—as in the George Blanchard House (pages 233, 234)—being original to the structure. In many cases these early examples can be identified by the use of a bolection moulding around the arched top or along the sides of the opening. In other cases, what was originally a very simple and primitive design, has been later supplemented by pilasters or other extensions, until it has become more pretentious,—and its actual age and integrity somewhat obscured in the process.

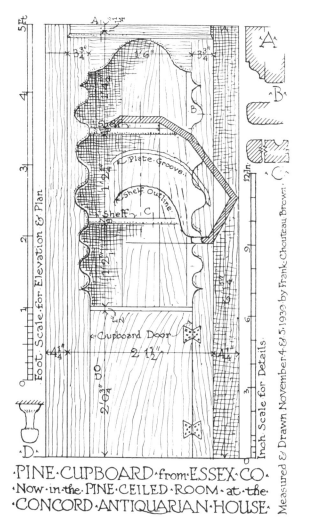

·PINE·CUPBOARD·from·ESSEX·CO·
·Now·in·the·PINE·CEILED·ROOM·at·the·
·CONCORD·ANTIQUARIAN·HOUSE·

where it now shows of less height than the ceiling of the room where it is located. To the writer's knowledge, just half of the cupboards here illustrated came from other houses than those in which they are now located. But their removal often has been the cause of their preservation down to the present day,—and—in nearly every case—they are still being preserved in a location near the site of their origin,—and often by descendants of the very families to whom they originally belonged!

Detail, Elevation View of Shell Top of Pine Corner Cupboard
WIGGIN-MILLER HOUSE, STRATHAM, NEW HAMPSHIRE

The example on page 228, for instance, speaks eloquently of its early date, and yet sometimes the primitive simplicity of such a design has been evolved, under similar conditions of remoteness from larger cities, at a much later period.

It should be remembered that, because of the decorative and appealing character of the corner cupboard, it has very often been separated from its original place of building. A family sells an old homestead, but reserves a mantel or two, as well as their old corner cupboard. As a rule, the earliest cupboards were built for houses with low ceilings; and consequently, when a cupboard is of somewhat lesser height than the room of which it is now a part,—one may suspect it to have been originally built for another house than that in which it is now placed. Of course, that must always be the case when they are preserved in some museum or historical society,—although that fact will also the more generally guarantee the authenticity of their local origin. In so many instances has the corner cupboard been transposed from its original to another location, that it is unreliable to expect its date to be the same as that of the house in which it may now be placed.

That this is not always the case, is proved by the cupboard in the Norton House at Annisquam (pages 237 and 240), which was found by the present owners built into one of the upstairs room corners, and removed by them—for greater usefulness—to the lower story,—

Frances and Mary Allen

Corner Cupboard
OLD MANSE, DEERFIELD, MASSACHUSETTS

Straight-Top Wall Cupboard Without Upper Doors
McCREERY HOUSE, CORNWALL, NEW YORK

Straight-Top Corner Cupboard with Paneled Doors
COL. ALEXANDER FIELD HOUSE, LONGMEADOW, MASS.

Early Corner Cupboard with Open-Arched Top
JABEZ WILDER HOUSE, HINGHAM, MASSACHUSETTS

Recessed Wall Cupboard with Open-Arched Top
TIMOTHY WOOD HOUSE, HALIFAX, MASSACHUSETTS

Open Corner Cupboard with Scalloped Semi-Circular Top
DANIELS HOUSE, SOMERS, CONNECTICUT

Open Corner Cupboard with Scalloped Semi-Circular Top
DANIEL GOULD HOUSE, BOXFORD, MASSACHUSETTS

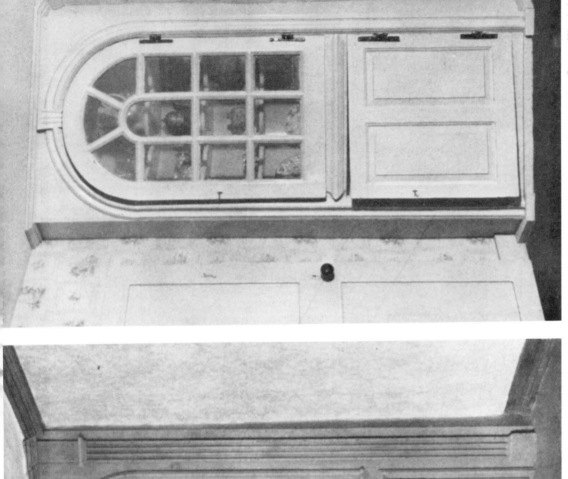

Courtesy Historic American Buildings Survey

Early Corner Cupboard with Glazed Semi-Circular-Top Door
GEORGE BLANCHARD HOUSE, MEDFORD, MASSACHUSETTS

Pine Open Corner Cupboard with Shell Top
WIGGIN-MILLER HOUSE, STRATHAM, NEW HAMPSHIRE

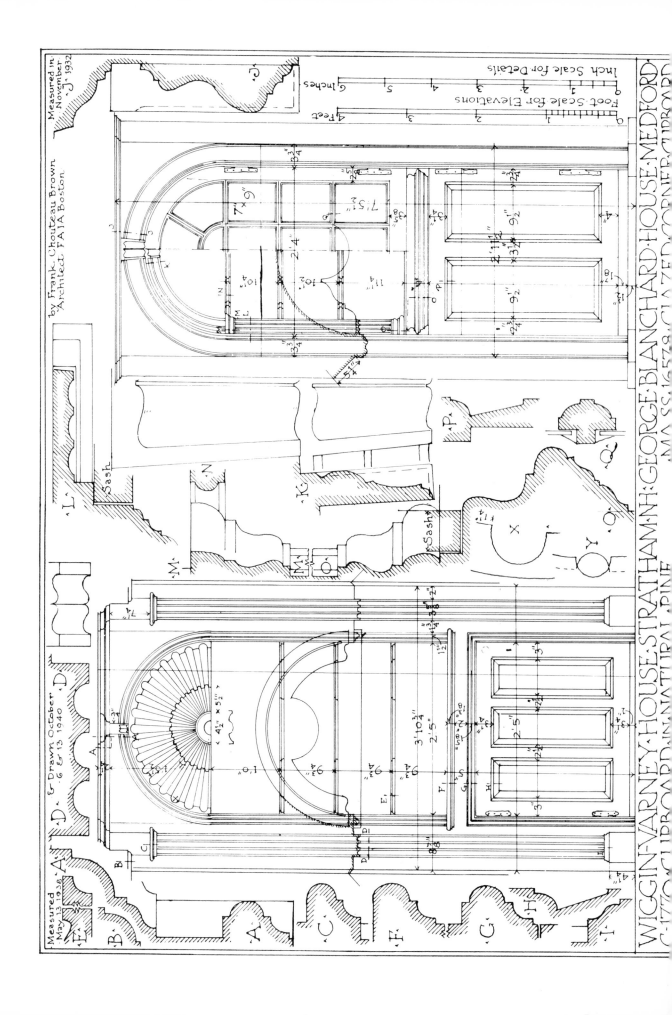

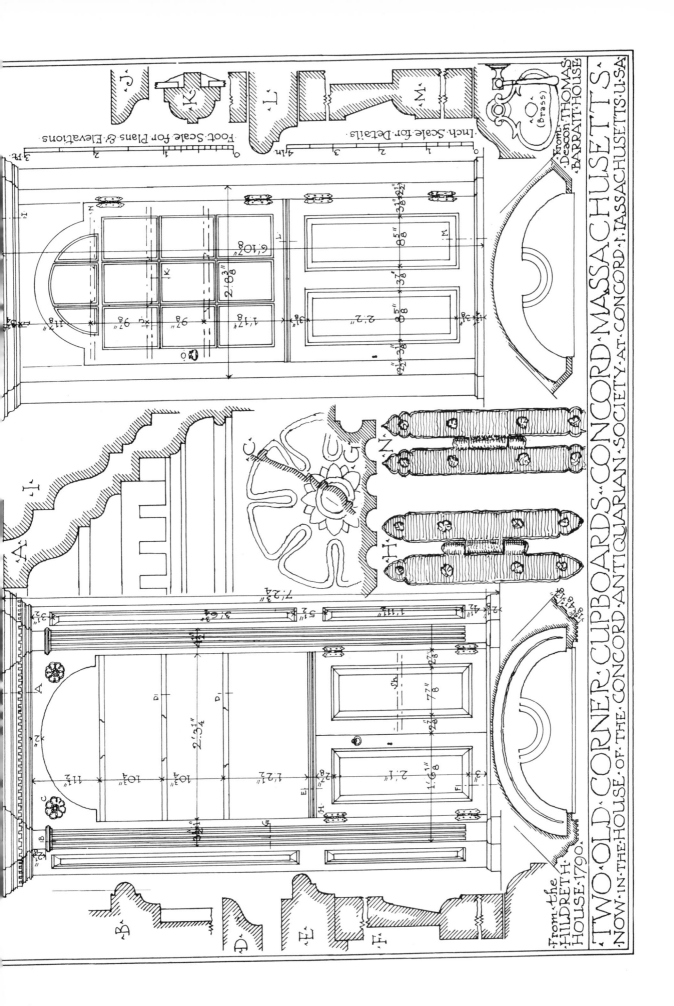

·TWO·OLD·CORNER·CUPBOARDS··CONCORD·MASSACHUSETTS·

·NOW·IN·THE·HOUSE·OF·THE·CONCORD·ANTIQUARIAN·SOCIETY·AT·CONCORD·MASSACHUSETTS·U·S·A·

·From·the
·Deacon·THOMAS·
·BARRATT·HOUSE·

·From·the
·HILDRETH·
·HOUSE·1790·

Foot·Scale·for·Plans·&·Elevations

Inch·Scale·for·Details

·O·
(Brass)

Now in Concord Antiquarian House

Corner Cupboard with Circle Top Glazed Door

DEACON THOMAS BARRATT HOUSE, CONCORD, MASS.

Now in Concord Antiquarian House

Open Corner Cupboard with Segment-Arched Top

HILDRETH HOUSE, CONCORD, MASSACHUSETTS

Pine Corner Cupboard with Open Semi-Circular Top
NORTON HOUSE, ANNISQUAM, MASSACHUSETTS

Pine Corner Cupboard with Open Semi-Circular Top
WILLIAM HASKELL HOUSE, WEST GLOUCESTER, MASS.

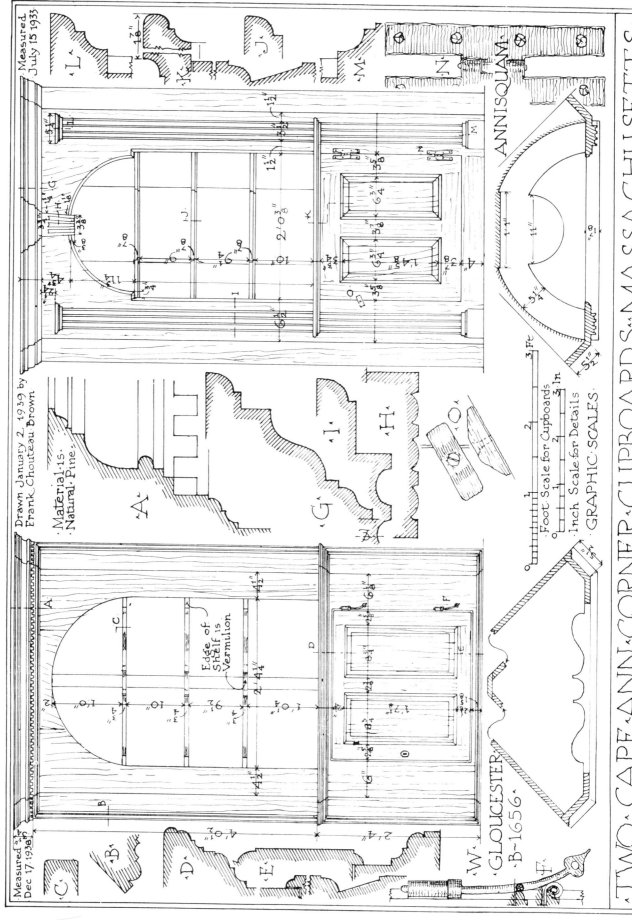

Measured
July 15 1933.

Drawn January 2 1939 by
Frank Chouteau Brown

Material is
Natural Pine.

Measured
Dec 17 1938.

Edge of
Shelf is
Vermilion

·ANNISQUAM·

·GLOUCESTER·
·B~1656·

Foot Scale for Cupboards
Inch Scale for Details
·GRAPHIC·SCALES·
3 Ft
3 In

·TWO·CAPE·ANN·CORNER·CUPBOARDS,·MASSACHUSETTS·

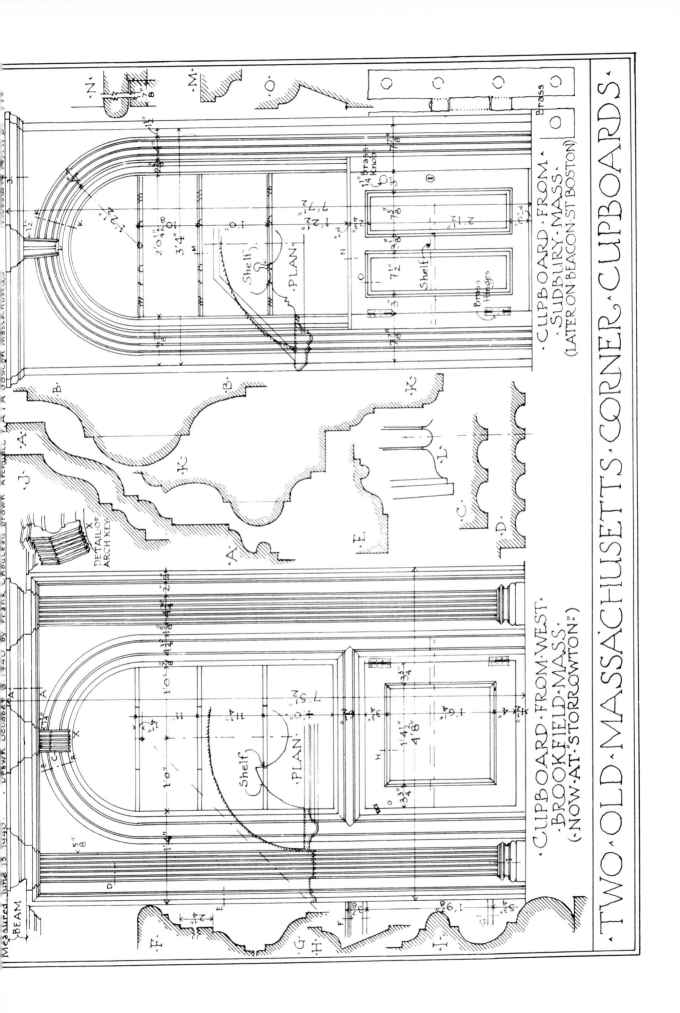

·TWO·OLD·MASSACHUSETTS·CORNER·CUPBOARDS·

·CUPBOARD·FROM·WEST·
·BROOKFIELD·MASS·
·(NOW·AT·"STORROWTON·")·

·CUPBOARD·FROM·
·SUDBURY·MASS·
(LATER·ON·BEACON·ST·BOSTON)

Open Corner Cupboard, Now in Phillips House,
"Storrowton," Massachusetts

Open Corner Cupboard, Now in Gilbert House,
"Storrowton," Massachusetts

GLOSSARY

ABACUS. Crowning member of a capital. It varies with order used. In a Doric capital, it is a flat rectangular slab, square in plan that rests between the echinus block of the capital and the lowest member of the entablature above.

ANCHOR. A wrought iron bar fastened to a beam end and built into a brick or stone wall, or sometimes carried through the wall and secured by a cross-iron in the shape of an S.

ARCHITRAVE. The lowest member of a classical entablature. A molded lintel spanning between columns.

ARCHIVOLT. The moulding of an architrave that is carried around the face of an arch.

ASTRAGAL. A small half-round moulding. It generally has a fillet on one or both sides.

BACK BAND. The outer moulding of a door or window.

BAR. A small moulded piece of glass used to separate the panes of glass in a sash.

BARGE BOARD. An often ornamented board that conceals and protects the roof timbers projecting over gables.

BATTEN. A board, either narrow or wide, nailed on the back of two or more other boards to hold them together. It seals or reinforces the joint.

BED MOULD. A moulding beneath the soffit, modillion band, or dentil band of a cornice.

BOLECTION MOULDING. A heavy moulding located partly on the panel and partly on the stile of panelwork. It projects beyond the general surface of the panel.

BRACKET. A curved or angular projection at the top of a post that enables it to support two or three beams. Produces a ledge-like element such as the eaves of a roof or a hood over a window. Frequently used for ornamental as well as structural purposes.

CAPITAL. The crowning member of a column or pilaster.

CASEMENT WINDOWS. Windows that open from the side on hinges, like doors, out from the plane of the wall.

CASTING. The mouldings or flat strip around a door or window on the inside.

CAVETTO. A hollow quarter-circle or quarter-ellipse moulding.

CHAIR RAIL. A moulding at chair height carried around a room to prevent chairbacks from damaging the wall plastering when placed against it.

CHAMFER. The oblique surface made by cutting off a square corner at an angle to each face.

CLAPBOARD. A thin board approximately four feet in length riven radially.

CONSOLE. A scroll-shaped bracket supporting a shelf or cornice.

COPING. The cap or top course of a wall, usually designed to shed water and often ornamental.

CORBEL. To build outward, by projecting successive courses of masonry beyond those below.

CORBELED CORNICE. A cornice made up of several projections each of which extends farther outward than the one below.

CORNICE. The crowning member of an entablature. Also, the mouldings of wood and plaster at the angle of wall and ceiling in a room or at the edge of a roof.

CORONA. The projecting part of a classic cornice.

CROSSETTE. A double mitering of the architrave at the upper corner of a door or window or other opening.

CYMATIUM. The crowning member of a cornice generally in the form of a cyma, so called from its contour resembling that of a wave.

DADO. The plain space in a pedestal between the base and the surbase. The lower part of an interior wall when especially decorated or faced; the decoration adorning this part of the wall.

DENTIL. A small ornamental block forming one of a series set in a row. A dentil molding is comprised of such a series.

DORMER WINDOW. A window in a sloping roof, with vertical sides and front.

DOVETAIL. The end of a beam cut into a truncated wedge to prevent it from pulling out of the framing.

ECHINUS. The ovolo moulding next below the abacus of the capital of a column.

ENGLISH BOND. Brickwork in the colonies was laid in two methods, both traditional to English architecture. In English bond, the bricks are set in alternating courses of stretchers (bricks laid across the length of the wall with their long side showing) and headers (bricks laid across the wall with their short end showing). In Flemish bond, the stretchers and headers alternate in the same row. This creates a more animated texture than English bond and was favored in the more elegant buildings.

ENTABLATURE. The top member of a classic order, being a richly molded continuous lintel supported on columns. It is divided horizontally into three main parts; the uppermost is the *cornice*, the middle one the *frieze*, and the lowest the *architrave*. Each has the moldings and decorative treatment of the particular order.

ENTASIS. A slight convexity of the shaft of the column.

ESCUTCHEONS. A protective or ornamental shield, as around a keyhole.

FAÇADE. An elevation or exterior front of a building, especially the principal or entrance front.

FASCIA. A flat horizontal member of an order or building having the form of a flat board.

FEATHEREDGED. An edge that is sharp and triangular in section. Usually found in one side of a clapboard or in the sides of a panel or of a sheathing board.

FENESTRATION. The arrangement in a building of its windows, especially the more important or larger ones.

FESTOONS. A carved or molded ornament representing a festoon of flowers, fruits, or leaves, wound with a ribbon and hanging in a natural curve.

FILLET. A small square member between two mouldings or between a moulding and a wider flat surface.

FINIAL. An ornament placed upon the apex of an architectural feature, such as a gable, turret, or canopy.

FLEMISH BOND. *See* ENGLISH BOND

FRET. A pattern jig-sawed out of thin wood and applied to a surface.

FRIEZE. Any long and narrow horizontal architectural member, especially one which has a chiefly decorative purpose. In Greek, Roman, and Neoclassical architecture it is that horizontal band which forms the central, and usually the most important, part of the entablature.

FURRING. Thin strips of wood used to bring the faces of joists or studs into line with each other.

GABLE. A triangular-shaped piece of wall closing the end of a double pitched roof.

GAMBREL ROOF. A roof that has a double pitch. The lower plane, which rises from the eaves, is rather steep; the upper plane, which spans from the lower to the ridgepole, has a flatter pitch.

GIRT. A principal horizontal beam in braced frame construction, such as a chimney girt or end girt.

GORGE. A hollow moulding, the same as the cavetto.

GUTTAE. One of a series of ornaments in the Doric entablature that is usually in the form of small drops of water.

HEAD. The lintel or top-piece of a door or window frame.

HEADERS. A brick laid with its end face to the weather. *See* ENGLISH BOND

HIPPED ROOF. A roof that pitches inward from all four sides. The external angle formed where an end plane and side plane meet is called the hip.

HIP-GAMBREL ROOF. A combination of a gambrel and a hip roof with the two small gables of the gambrel.

JAMB. An upright surface forming the side of a window or door frame, of an opening in a wall, or of a fireplace.

LEAN-TO. A room or line of rooms with a roof which seems to lean against a larger mass. A house with such a roof at its back.

LIGHTS. The panes of glass in a window, such as eight-light, six-light or twelve-light.

LINTEL. The horizontal structural member which supports the wall over an opening or spans between two adjacent piers or columns.

METOPE. In a Doric entablature, that part of the frieze which falls between two triglyphs. In the Greek Doric order the metope characteristically contains sculpture.

MODILLION CORNICE. A cornice supported by a series of small ornamental brackets under the projecting, top moldings. It is common to the Corinthian and Composite orders.

MORTISE AND TENON JOINT. A joint which is made by one member having its end cut in a projecting piece (tenon) which fits exactly into a groove or hole (mortise) in the other member. Once joined, the pieces are held together by a peg which passes through the tenon.

MOULDING. An ornamental shaping of the internal or external angles or surfaces or of the faces of a beam board, or other solid, or of a group of these, into forms copied from stonework.

MULLION. An upright post or similar member

dividing a window into two or more units, or lights, each of which may be further subdivided into panes.

MUNTINS. *See* MULLION

MUTULES. Projecting inclined blocks in the Doric cornices, derived from the ends of wooden beams.

ORDER. The most important elements of classical architecture are the orders, first developed as a structural-aesthetic system by the ancient Greeks. An order has two major components. A column with its capital forms the post, or main vertical supporting member. The principal horizontal member is the entablature, or lintel. The entablature consists of three horizontal parts. The lowest one is the architrave, an unbroken horizontal element which rests directly on the capitals and forms the principal part of the lintel. Above this is a second horizontal area called the frieze, which is generally decorated with sculptural ornament. The top member is the cornice; made up of various combinations of moldings, it overhangs the rest of the entablature and becomes the crowning motif. On the gabled end of a building, the cornice is continued up along the edge of the roof (now called a raking cornice) to form an enclosed triangle, or pediment. In classical architecture, the roof planes were pitched at a moderate angle, making the pediment a low, wide equilateral triangle. The Greeks developed three different types of orders, the Doric, Ionic, and Corinthian, each distinguishable by its own decorative system and proportions.

OVERHANG. The projection of an upper part of a building beyond the lower part.

OVOLO. The quarter-round moulding.

PALLADIAN WINDOW. An arrangement in which a round-headed window is flanked by lower square-headed openings and separated from them by columns or pilasters.

PANEL. A board planed to a featheredge, then set into a frame of stiles and rails.

PANEL BACK. A panel under a window sill, inside the house.

PEDIMENT. The low triangular gable formed by the roof slopes on top and the horizontal enclosing member, generally a cornice, beneath.

PILASTER. The projecting part of a square column which is attached to a wall; it is finished with the same cap and base as a freestanding column. Also a narrow vertical member in a similar position.

PIN. A round piece of wood used to fasten mortises and tenons together.

PLINTH. The lowest member of a base; a sub-base; a block upon which the moldings of an architrave or trim are stopped at the bottom.

PORTECOCHERE. A large gateway allowing vehicles to drive into a courtyard.

PORTICO. A porch consisting of a low-pitched roof supported on classical columns and finished in front with an entablature and pediment.

QUIRK. A cutting back of the upper part of a moulding under the fillet.

QUOIN. The bricks or stones laid in alternating directions, which bond and form the exterior corner angle of a wall.

RABBET. A rectangular sinkage at the corner of a piece of framing or finish, generally to receive another piece joined thereto.

RAIL. The vertical framing member which tenons into the stile.

RAKE. *See* ORDER

REGULI. A short band, under the triglyphs of the Doric entablature, and to which the guttae are attached. (Generally, a surface that serves as a base for figures.)

RIDGEPOLE. The board or plank at the apex of a roof against which the upper ends of the rafters abut.

SASH WINDOWS. Windows with frames that slide vertically up and down in a grooved frame. In contrast with CASEMENT WINDOWS they open within the plane of the wall.

SHIPLAPPING. Shaving the ends of clapboards and bevelling the edges of outside boarding to keep out water.

SKIRT. An apron piece or border, as a baseboard or the molded piece under a window stool.

SOFFIT. The underside of a subordinate part and member of buildings such as staircases, entablatures, archways, and cornices.

STILE. One of the upright pieces in framing or paneling; one of the primary members of a frame into which the rail tenons.

STRETCHER. A brick laid with its long face to the weather. *See* ENGLISH BOND.

SUMMER BEAM. In early New England braced frame construction, a large horizontal beam which runs from the chimney girt at right angles to the end girt in the outer frame, at a point opposite to the chimney.

TRANSOM. A horizontal bar, as distinguished from a mullion; especially one crossing a door or window opening near the top.

TRIGLYPH. One of the vertical blocks in a Doric frieze, suggesting in stone, the outer ends of the ceiling beams that were used in primitive wooden construction. It has three narrow vertical elements which form two triangular channels.

TYMPANUM. The triangular wall of a pediment between its enclosing moldings, frequently ornamented with sculpture. The similarly placed wall over a square-headed door or window which is set in an arch.

VOUSSOIR. A wedge-shaped stone or brick used in the construction of an arch. Its taper toward the center is made to coincide with radii of the arch.